100 Select Poems *plus* one ~ Martina Reisz Newberry

100
Select Poems
plus
one

Martina Reisz Newberry

inner child press, ltd

100 Select Poems *plus* one ~ Martina Reisz Newberry

General Information

100 Select Poems plus One
Martina Reisz Newberry

1st Edition : January 2012

This Publishing is protected under Copyright Law as a "Collection". All rights for all submissions are retained by the Individual Artist and / or Poet. No part of this Publishing may be Reproduced, Transferred in any manner without the prior **WRITTEN CONSENT** of the "Material Owner" or it's Representative Inner Child Press.

Any such violation infringes upon the Creative and Intellectual Property of the Owner pursuant to International and Federal Copyright Law.
Any queries pertaining to this "Collection" should be addressed to Publisher of Record.

Publisher Information

1st Edition : Inner Child Press :
innerchildpress@gmail.com
www.innerchildpress.com

This Collection is protected under U.S. and International Copyright Laws

Copyright © 2011 : Martina Reisz Newberry
Filed by : Inner Child Press

Cover Photography :   Darko Kotevski
                                Calla11" from the series CALLAS/KALE
                                http://darkophotography.yolasite.com/

Cover Designs :   William S. Peters, Sr.

ISBN-13 :0615569390
ISBN-10 :9780615569390

$ 21.95 US

100 Select Poems *plus* one ~ Martina Reisz Newberry

Acknowledgements

Grateful acknowledgement is made to the following journals in which some of these poems first appeared:

Health Plan, Yet Another Small Magazine
No Hay Banda, Pedestal Magazine
Salutations and Prostrations, Arabesques War and Poetry Anthology
Praise, Saxifrage Press
Bad Manners, Cenacle Magazine
Postures, Best Poems Encyclopedia
All that Jazz and *Bad Manners*, Trivia Magazine.

Additional thanks to the following journals for their support of my work over the last 30 years:

5 AM, Amelia, Ascent Aspirations, Bellingham Review, Black Buzzard Review, Cape Rock, Caprice, Catalyst, Connecticut Poetry Review, Context South, Current Accounts, Descant, Haight Ashbury Literary Journal, Hob Nob, i.e., Innisfree, Iota, Iowa Woman, The Ledge, New Laurel Review, Passages North, Piedmont Literary Review, Snake Nation Review, Sonoma Mandala, Sonora Review, Rectangle, Southern Review of Poetry, Touchstone, Visions International, Willow Review, Yet Another Small Magazine,

100 Select Poems *plus* one ~ Martina Reisz Newberry

100 Select Poems *plus* one ~ Martina Reisz Newberry

Dedication

Larry Kramer

Poet, Brother, Teacher, Friend ...

I miss you.

100 Select Poems *plus* one ~ Martina Reisz Newberry

Author's Note

My publishing record is a little gawky and somewhat untidy, though colorful. There are a number of books and a chapbook published, all of which I love and which exemplify my passion for poems. I have edited the selected poems in this book by dismantling previous collections. They are presented in sequence by the titles in which they first appeared and, in that way, the book is its own story.

My unconscious models for the construction of these poems have been *Selected Poems of Norman Dubie* and *A.R. Ammons Collected Poems* both of which have provided a definitive influence on my life and work. I mention them because their work is so different and, at the same time, similar to mine. This is not to say that they are my only influences. There are so many other brilliant "ghosts," talented minds I appeal to when trying to put my particular way of experiencing the world to paper. So, I thank them all and include in that thanks my publishers, past and present.

Martina Reisz Newberry

100 Select Poems *plus* one ~ Martina Reisz Newberry

Table of Contents

plus *one*

Celebration	3

from . . . **Running Like A Woman With Her Hair On Fire**

Links	7
The Orchard	8
A Reckoning	9
The Woman Who Read The Bible	10
Thinking About What Might Happen	12
On The First Day Of October	13
Something I Know About	14
James Dean's Shadow	15
Gay Repartee	16
Kiss Of The Vampire	18
John To The Seven Churches	19
When You Saw Her, You Knew	20
Atlas	21
About The Day You Were Born	22
You Can Never Be Sure	24
Hearst Beach—San Simeon	25
Balm In Gilead	26

Table of Contents . . . continued

from . . . **Not Untrue And Not Unkind**

At The Polish Club	29
Shadow Puppets	30
Encounter With A Riparian Understory	31
No Hay Banda	32
Neutrinos	34
Lost Causes	36
Another Cinco De Mayo . . . And I Still Don't Know What I'm Celebrating	37
Go Away, I'm Cleaning	39
Supernatural Episodes	40
Local Color	42
And Back Again	43
With The Koi	44
A Certain Relief	46
Aftershock	47
"Women Buy Clothes As A Form Of Prayer To A God Never Satisfied By Offered Flesh"	48

Table of Contents . . . continued

from . . . **After The Earthquake**

Salutations And Prostrations	51
Fall Air Tastes Like Whiskey	53
Awakenings	55
Until Dark	57
Several Years After Your Death	59
Epistle To The Romans	60
Rapture II	62
Health Plan	63
Symptoms	64
Fourteen Miles Outside The Cape Of The Poor Clares, A Name I Invented	66
Letter To An Old Friend	67
Sparrow Hawk Season	69
Drinking Wine Right From The Bottle	71
The Angry Affirmative	72
The Big Couch	73
The Full Moon Rises	75

Table of Contents . . . continued

from . . . **Hunger**

All That Jazz	79
Planning A Convenient Future	80
What We Did	82
Before The Fall	85
Call Waiting	87
Insomnia	88
Your Mother Weeps In The Mezzanine	90
Intention	92
Glass	93
Black Velvet	95
"Ghosts Seem Harder To Please Than We Are…"	97
Gin And Tonic In Charlotte	99
Enhancement And A Red Moon	100
February 20, 2006	101
Patriot	103
Bi-Visiblet	105
That Which Separates Us From Lentils	108
Sonata For Three Violins And A Kazoo With Signs Following	110

Table of Contents . . . continued

from . . . **Perhaps You Could Breathe For Me**

Requests	113
Study Of Trees	114
In The Kitchen	116
60-Something Female Poet Writing To Her Country In The First Decade Of A New Millennium	117
Praise	118
Philosophy	119
4 P..M.	120
Beautiful	121
Ashes	125
Postures	126
The Looming Whatever	128
The Hang Of Happiness	129
For Real	131
Boulevard	132
The Ugly Building On A Hot Day	133
Bad Manners	134

Table of Contents . . . continued

from . . . **Late Night Radio**

Unidentified Flying Objects	139
Lucid Dreaming	140
The Number Of The Beast	141
Lost Civilizations: Chernobyl, April 1986	143
Conspiracies, It Might Be Best Not To Listen	145
Chakra-Ajna (Brow)	146
Wicca-The Ovaries Of War	147
Remote Viewing	148
Druids	149
The Fate Of Consciousness	151
The Existence Of The Ten Realms Of Being	152
Channeling	153

Table of Contents . . . continued

from . . . **What We Can't Forgive**

Collateral Damage	157
"… I Feel Myself A Cog In Somethin' Turning."	158
What Madness Is	159
A Thousand Signs	160
Unraveling The Day	162
Untitled	163

Epilogue

Publications	**167**
Video Production	**168**
Achievements	**169**
Reviews	**170**
Acknowledgments	**171**

Forward

It was in 1988, or maybe 1989; a long time ago, now, that Martina Newberry was standing at a wooden rail looking down across long, rolling, green slopes toward the ocean when I happened to look out the window from the kitchen to see her standing there. We were at Djerassi Artists Residents Program in Northern California.

Dear reader, please let me step away for just a moment. I am not a poet, not one who writes. I am a photographer. I want you to know this as you read my very slight observations. I feel the depth of the universe when I look at something, and when that thing's surface convinces me by its appearances in the world.

When read Martina's work, I enter it not by following the words, but by what my senses bring me, through those words. My eye follows less those words and more the line down the page Martina crafts from them.

That moment so many years ago of catching Martina, the person standing outdoors, taking in that long view from the Skyline ridge down to the ocean at San Gregorio is fading in my memory. I remember certain energetic warmth, the beating heart which touches me in her poetry. Martina stood out on the deck that day, and I walked out to join her, to share that moment in fellowship with her, looking out across that landscape.
In her poems is that very invitation, reoffered in myriad imagery.

One theme in this poetry is that of loss crossed by discovery, and of the heart enduring, albeit suspended between desire and fulfillment. On that long-ago afternoon, that great light-flecked space in the landscape before us might have reminded one of what might be, or of fleeting fulfillments which will come, even if not invited nor expected.

100 Select Poems *plus* one ~ Martina Reisz Newberry

Forward . . . *continued*

A certain force in Martina's poetry seems to derive from slightly twisting imagery like this, as, in the poem *Neutrinos*, we are reminded of events which touch us but which may not register. So may it be with love, in these poems which remind us we may be the wiser without knowing it.

As with taking in the light and the land shape that afternoon, these poems need to be seen in space, not simply viewed on the page: read out loud. To hear these lines successive images come forth. Even that, for this reader, is not their real source. More than projecting imagery the poems amalgamate image, sound, and discursive flow. Description comes forth, a tactile palpable flow. For this reader this is the catalyst for an
emotion that resolves into a "Yes" for life, for heart.

Might a love poem pass through me, yet I not feel a thing? Would love? Perhaps these poems, for whatever deadpan sincerity they affect, contain yet a dram of classic irony. To read them now, or then, may be enough: tincture of time will take care of the rest.

Bob Tyson

Photographer
Turin, Italia
13 November 2011

100 Select Poems *plus* one ~ Martina Reisz Newberry

Namaste'

100
Select Poems
plus
one

Martina Reisz Newberry

inner child press, ltd

100 Select Poems *plus* one ~ Martina Reisz Newberry

plus

one

100 Select Poems *plus* one ~ Martina Reisz Newberry

Celebration

The morning's birthday rang through us like
a gong. Outside, no one believed there
was such a thing as mortality

and there was a perpetual grin
on the windshields of the cars down
in the street. Someone may have been

dreaming us, but we hoped they would not
wake up; our happiness was that
feral. We were safe and slipped into

the day on the remnants of last night's
moon. Over glasses of tea, we read
each other's palms to see where we were

going, but we could see only that
there is more than one truth in this world.
The morning's birthday showed us where to

how to begin the celebration,
where to put our things and where to go out
so that others could come in and find ease.

100 Select Poems *plus* one ~ Martina Reisz Newberry

100 Select Poems *plus* one ~ Martina Reisz Newberry

from

Running Like A Woman With Her Hair On Fire

Red Hen Press ~ 2005

100 Select Poems *plus* one ~ Martina Reisz Newberry

Links

Expatriation: three girls,
children really, running-not looking back.
One thinks of tidying her room.
One thinks of a grilled cheese sandwich.
The third thinks of the boy back there
in the trees, of his hands, his moans
extinguishing the bird sounds.
"Run!" she screams to those two behind her.
"Run faster. Don't look behind you."
Which one was I?
Which one were you?
That evening, remembering, you said,
"Don't forget. We promised never to tell."
Tell me something covert-even if it's a lie.
Tell me: where you were when John Kennedy's ear blew off.
Tell me: how you observed the place of your lost gods.
Tell me: who you were in bed with then? Was he/she living in
your eyes, your throat?
Tell me: what were your darkest impulses in those days?
What did you make stronger and what did you endure?
Were you ready then, as in the wind of your daughter's hands,
your son's laughter, for the difficult contours of this earth?
The phone rings and rings in this empty room.
I will never regret not answering it.
Did you wish to be broken?
Did I?

The Orchard

We visited Aunt at her house with the
cement porch and the acre of apricot trees.
Our mothers and fathers said, "Be careful,
"stay clean." Aunt said, "Now don't rile the bees."
Cousin Lou, Cousin Pauline, Cousin Craig, and me
wandered as far into those trees as we dared,
then took off our shoes to step on overripe,
fallen fruit. Lou kissed Pauline and dared Craig
to kiss me, but he wouldn't answer the dare,
only led me further into the trees
until we found a clear place to sit where
we could see Lou and Pauline pressing themselves
against each other, mouths open, tongues working.
"They oughtn't," I said, "it's wrong." Cousin Craig
bit his lip and pulled my hair. "Don't worry,"
he said, "it's ok as long as it doesn't
'rile the bees.'" They called us to come back then.

We stared at the sound their voices made.
A fury overtook us as we
started back-a rage. We picked up apricots,
as many as we could, began running,
throwing them everywhere, running with our hands
in the air, shouting and crying out
as if the sky were on fire. "We're here!
We're coming! We're here!"

A Reckoning

Minds break almost
in the same way a heart does.
It just takes longer.
Even when a heart stops
expecting, stops waiting,
for sleep or peace or the
contrite word, the mind
does not. It stays alert,
on the job. It takes
the photographs, puts forth
the reasonable explanation:
Soon, the mind says, *when
he has rested, when it is
cooler, when it is morning…*
The heart has given up
by this time, has broken,
is shattered. But the mind turns
away from its own distraction.
It refuses to notice
the danger: the exposed root,
the shards of glass, the blown fuse.
when, at last, these things are irrefutable,
it breaks. Just like a heart-
almost exactly like a heart.

The Woman Who Read The Bible

She would get out the Bible.
On an afternoon sometimes,
Mother would get it from
the top shelf of the big
mahogany bookcase.
It wasn't faith she was looking for
among the prophets and poets.
Her mind wasn't right at those times.
She craved a louder voice than
those that wailed inside her head
and beat at her ears. It was
a quick stab at heaven
she wanted; thinking how it might go:
how she might turn a gilt-edged
page and a ray of brilliant light
would shoot forth from the words
and Jesus
Jesus would heal her then and there.

The Woman Who Read the Bible . . . *continued*

I was the little child who
would lead the savior to her.
I sat still as stagnant water while
she read almost inaudibly
those dreadful stories of miracles:
demons driven into a herd
of swine, a few loaves and fishes
feeding five thousand people,
Lazarus waking up from
death and leaving his grave like
some benign Boris Karloff.
My mother's voice bent and
broke. Finally silent,
she waited for God to see us
sitting side by side on the bed,
bathed in purity and
resolution. Almost shy,
she'd bow her head to whisper
"Amen," and get up unredeemed,
put the book away, and start dinner.

Thinking About What Might Happen

You thought about what might happen:
Contemplation of the Wheel-A Portrait
(You were framed.)
We went to buy books; your hands were busy
touching titles as if they were Braille.
Poetry by Touch, a nice concept.
Your mouth was set as if for chocolates
or custard. Consider what was done:
how you smoothed the pages and your fingers
moved, danced-fast as coyotes over
the words. What if. . .what if. . . what if I
had been a whore and not who you know
at all? What if my name was Babylon
and I pulled sentences over my legs
like stockings?
Ah! Bow your head now-hope that, this once,
the night won't be dark.

On The First Day Of October

When I learned to tie my shoes,
I always stopped at the same place.
You know that place where the lace
goes around itself, right before the bow
is born. I always stopped right there,
frozen. Time went nowhere, birds stopped
flying, dogs stopped scratching. It was
like a photograph of a bicycle rider-
you can see that he should be moving,
but the picture has caught him in the place
he will be forever: one knee raised, ready
to push down on the pedal.
There is so much one needs to go on through
to all that is waiting. In the case of
shoelace tying, it is courage; in the case
of bicycle riding, it is coordination;
in the case of loving, it is vision.
I once left a friend in San Rafael
who wrote to me. She said: *"I can't believe
how small I have become. I have been
reduced by events, surprised, hurt without
reason, artfully carved up."*

I don't know. . . check with me later
for the things you need to know.
We can talk about them sometime
when the coffee is poured and too hot to drink;
maybe on the first day of October
when we find just the smallest bit of ice
on the car windshield.

Something I Know About

You inhale the certain grassy smell,
note the towel blowing soft on the line.
"Yes," you nod, *"it will be clear today;
and there is the cat and there an owl."*
You clearly understand, for the moment,
how things are. But, inside, where your hunger sits,
are vital sounds wicked as meteors.
Each small thing competes for its own realness:
A child hugs himself to sleep, a snake
naps in the warm roadway, some tall creature
bends to come in your door,
and, subtler than waking from a nap,
you will go back to where you began,
disposed toward another way of loving.

James Dean's Shadow

My father used to say: *Not everyone casts a shadow.*
I believed it was one of those things adults say; one of
those things only deciphered after you reach thirty and
are allowed to understand everything. You've heard
A-Wink-Is-As-Good-As-A-Nod-To-A-Blind-Horse?
At 67, I'm still not sure what that means.
But shadows...shadows are different. Nobody talks about them.
Though they are faithful, staying with the guy that brought them,
shadows get little attention. This is also true of God.
God is different than he used to be. He notices less now.

Once, it was up to God whether or not you got a shadow,
or kept it once you had it. Now, it's haphazard.
My father had one, so did my favorite uncle. My mother
and her sister each had one. Mother's was long and thin
and preceded her down the hall at bedtime. Aunt Ersta's
was round and mean. You never saw it coming. I am certain
I started out with one, then lost it somewhere and it has
remained lost, unless, of course, it was found by God and
reassigned-the way they reassigned James Dean's shadow
after his horrible car accident. You remember. . .

Gay Repartee

Sit with me; I want to explain something:
I've always tended to myself, taken care of
my own needs-"only" children are like that.
We get overlooked in the long run
and we do not mind it.
In my stucco house, I read books,
played with make-believe brothers and sisters;
I kept the radio volume low and spoke
when spoken to. There was grace in the world then.
I cultivated a soft voice and a gentle nature.
I learned generosity from a neighbor lady
who shared pomegranates with us.
I learned a cheery outlook from
the Downs Syndrome boy my mother babysat.
I learned how to cook from
the Lebanese woman across the alley.
"What smells good, tastes good," she said.
Believe it. I smell as good as anything
that ever came out of my kitchen.
When I turned 12, a family friend told me I was homely,
said it was time I *learned something about life*,
said no other man would want me, probably,
then bedded and beat me for two years running.
Who knew to tell a grownup? (They don't like surprises.)
"I'm sorry," I said when my mother found out. "I'm sorry,"
I said when my daddy asked why.
A husband put marks on me that turned
my body into a roadmap.

Gay Repartee . . . *continued*

"I'm sorry," I told him, "to have made you so angry.
I'm sorry. I'll try harder to do what you want."
As he was pulling out of the driveway, in our only car,
he said I was the sorriest woman he'd ever known.
I considered how that was probably true.
His unkindness should have made me mean as swamp water,
but, no, I will give you anything that is mine to give.
This is something you know, dear love.
You are so good to look at, my tongue sticks
to the roof of my mouth, I get breathless.
What is it like for you to know that? I trudge ahead
with my best self in my open hands, trusting my
fine qualities to be enough for anyone. They
ought to be, yes? So why, then, do I find myself
living the same apology over and over,
running like a woman with her hair on fire?

Kiss Of The Vampire

In the movie, everything is in shades of gray
so that we understand about love being alive
even among the dead. Definitely a gray area.
When he takes her in his arms and she lets him
hold her like this and like this and then
he learns to like it that she worries about
his health and if he's taking his vitamins,
then the scary part really begins. I mean,
as long as he's just love-nipping her
on the throat and lips, it's okay,
but you know and I know-o god yes-we know
that she hasn't the faintest idea,
the foggiest notion, that this will be
the last love of her whole life.
She can't know that,
or she'd never ever ever do it.
Isn't that so?
Isn't it?

John To The Seven Churches

Write the things which thou hast seen, and the things which are, and the things which shall be hereafter. ~ Revelation 1:19

I am not doing good work.
Each day, I recede a little further.
I see who I was-standing
on an ice floe (which used to be
the Island of Blue Flowers)-
I wave as I sail away.
"Goodbye!" I shout to myself.
"Bear witness," I call out.
"Tell all who will listen
about the way it used to be.
Tell how the price becomes
dearer and dearer and how
all must run for high ground
because the waters rise
before you know it."
Back on the ice floe,
the woman who was me, nods
and smiles. "I will," she calls back.
"You can count on me."

When You Saw Her, You Knew . . .

She was the girl with the dark, curled hair
and the red wool coat. She was the girl
the boys chased and waited, impatient, to
push her on the swings.
She was the cheerleader with red hair
who got nine invitations to the
Hawaiian Dreams Dance, the girl who
would not say "hello" to you though she lived
only 2 houses down on your side of the street.
She was the blond in your German class who
never cracked a book and the tiny girl
in your Theater class whose black eyes
burned the boys to ash.
She was the brunette in your office
who wore micro-mini skirts, who fluttered
scarlet-tipped nails and never
had to pay for her own lunch.
You knew who she was the moment
your husband introduced her
and you knew-saw-the way
he smiled at her, saw the axe in his hand.

Atlas ... *because you love maps...*

You breathe in the night, slow and quiet:
once for me and once for yourself then catch
your breath, hoarding it like silver. Your feet
are warm against my legs. In summer
the dark is too hot and close and there is
such stillness...spidery dreams that stretch over
us like an unfinished argument.
Outside it is too quiet. even
the crickets sweat and sound cranky. Cats tango
on our trash can lids-foreplay, then angry
lovemaking then more dancing while I
listen and laugh and sleep again on sheets
like relief maps of distant countries.
In this dark, I am a light to no one
but myself. Somewhere a nightmare finds me;
you wake me up to talk a little and
it is almost as though a rainfall has begun.

About The Day You Were Born

Straggler, you broke through, but don't think how,
on the day you were born, the weather or
the news in the newspaper or the
television blatting away may have
placed no blessing on who you came to be.
Maybe that day was the day the whale got lost
in the bay outside San Francisco and
150 people put on their
slickers and jackets and went out to help it
find a way back to its birth canyons.
Or perhaps you were born on the day that
poor, sad woman had simply had enough
of being beaten so she set fire to the
bed there where her spouse slept, never fearing
God's wisdom or his own arrogant demise.
It's just one of those things no one thinks
about much. We remember the date, and
sometimes the time of day and sometimes
the name of the hospital, but seldom
do we think, "It was the day they finally
abandoned the rocket pads at Cape
Canaveral," or "It was the same day
of the month that poor Nat Turner was skinned."

About The Day You Were Born . . . *continued*

You might sit upstairs in the spare room and
look through an old suitcase at photos
and old letters. You might sit in the old
armchair up there nearly letting yourself
go to sleep with those pictures in your lap,
but, even with all of that, you won't say,
"I was born on the day that crazy
mimosa tree finally bloomed for the very
first time." You won't say it because the only
thing that really feels important is that you
were born, and the changes in the universe
are an entirely different thing indeed.

You Can Never Be Sure

It may be the tender turning
of this most fragile of planets,
or some bird's awful cry
so far away you can nearly
not hear it. The Possible
may change to the Impossible
right before your eyes.
I watched a field mouse run
like crazy from my garage,
(from inside the sack of birdseed,
I reckon), across the lawn
toward the bushes. He never made it.
A hawk got him mid-run.
Dying ruins everything,
and not just for field mice.
When I think of this, I am scattered
like hailstones. There are too many
possibilities, none with scientific
underpinnings. When I think of this,
just the very moves: the walk
to our pigeon house with the white
seed bucket; to sit on the linoleum
and make warm noises back at
the feather-footed birds;
to offer their breakfast on
the backs of my hands,
my lower lip, my crossed legs-
all this tells me it is too late
for warnings and I must make
my decisions now.

Hearst Beach - San Simeon

Walk as far as this small beach will take you,
to the end, to the warehouses; weathered
wood, blackened and holding back what they've seen.
Light plays there on splintered floors, ridicules
the broken windows and lets the ocean voice
sing through. Leave the sand behind you and climb
the stairs; they'll forgive your trespass. Shipload
after shipload was entertained at their doors.
Men worked here, raged and lifted, pushed against
packing crates, going home only when the holds
were empty and the holdings caged. Here are the
leavings of those whose hardened hands and
sympathies were the same. Withered warehouse
champions, fury long spent in these dirty,
sand-swept temples. They watch, they hunker and watch,
those who kept the cold waters to their promises.
Later, go back down to the sand the way
you came. Go back to your lunch and the gulls
and the rocks. Though you will be asked again and again,
you might never tell what has touched you and where.

Balm In Gilead

Clearly he had forgotten.
I smell like lilacs, I said,
like sandalwood. His memory
faltered, disturbed by static
and half visions. *I am full
of your sunsets,* I said.
*I am your navigator,
your blazing place.* He drew
a blank on that one. There was
wonder, but no recognition
in his face. *Think of
a picnic*, I told him, *with ants
and rain clouds and the white wine
turned warm and the croissants soggy.*
He shook his fair head. We were
not in Rotterdam or Paris.
A small tremor burst from
the San Andreas Fault.
The lamp and the mirror trembled.
I saw myself in the glass.
I am your Beautiful Loser
I said. His eyes threw sparks
all over the room.
He embraced me and cried.
"I KNEW YOU'D COME BACK."
He just kept saying that.

100 Select Poems *plus* one ~ Martina Reisz Newberry

from

Not Untrue
And Not Unkind

Arabesques Press ~ 2006

At The Polish Club

At the Polish Club, the ladies sit
with their skirts pushed up, stockings rolled.
They fan themselves with the bulletin from
St. Stephen's Parish and sip some sweet wine.
The older ones tell about Uncle Stash
who danced better than anyone ever
could though he was 5'3" tall and 235 lbs.;
finally died right there on the dance floor
in the middle of the "She's Too Fat For Me"
polka played as well as it ever was played
by Norbert Pulski and the South Lorain
Stompers -- the Stompers being made up of
Joe Kulak, Chester Sodowski, Len
Drozewski and Louise Lock who married
above herself and outside the church but
could sure play the drums even without her
right little finger which had gotten mashed
in a roll press when she was single and
still worked at the mill. Bill Lock didn't dance
at all, was not Polish, but came to the
Club to watch after Louise because she
had a "reputation" and needed
looking after. One night that Bill wasn't
there, she'd gone home with some guy from Amherst
who had a blue pickup truck. Bill came looking
for her, heard where she went and the next time
Norbert Pulski and the South Lorain Stompers
played, Louise was wearing an eye patch and
salve on her upper lip. After that, Bill
always came to stand at the bar, tap his foot,
and keep an eye on Louise who played her very best
the night Uncle Stash danced himself to death
right out there on the dance floor. Right out there.

Shadow Puppets

She cooked for them in the evening: green peas
and squash, some kind of meat and hard rolls.
A ritual of hands and eyes and
movements. Outside, the dark held up
the leaves of the camphor tree
like a silhouette artist about to begin cutting.
She thought of how much she wanted rain
and how much sweeter things would be if only
she could hear water dripping from the eaves.
In the kitchen, no one crowded around her.
The wine was the color of a riverbed;
she thought of trout, of pebbles, everything
shining, everything wet. She watched her hands
setting the table. Something whispered,
"This is real. Quickly, save yourself!"

Encounter With A Riparian Understory

Places ought to be kinder.   But here
is a delicateness that famishes
what heart is left in me; makes it chafe,
and my eyes and mouth liable to crying.
Rivers should not be so sweet--tentative
as this river is--nor trees as shy
as these oaks and bays. The air is slow
and quiet here, deferential to
a beauty horrendous in its power
to make me selfish and sad.
Whole trees across the trail; the temperature
up, down, up again, and the wind
gravely moves as if only the wind
knows how much wind is too much wind
to blow.

No Hay Banda . . . *There is no band. It is all an illusion.*
Spoken by **Bondar,** a character from the movie, Mulholland Drive

Don't look at me now.
Late fall is here and I'm tired of myself.
The room is full of colored pencils
but I use the same two pastels again and again.

I can't help it.
The November moon is a small hard stone
from which icy water falls and bathes
the sun in impossible gleamings.

Don't look at me.
I am soaked to the knees in loneliness
and angrier than I am clean.
This time of year tears at me,

makes me recount old tales to myself
without the comfort of reinvention.
My friend, who once guided me in all things,
died before I knew how crucial

was hypothesis, and excess,
before I saw that I was committed
to humility and the acceptance of everything.
Don't look at me now.

No Hay Banda . . . *continued*

Wait for godssakes
until the air is apple warm, pear warm.
Wait for variables, for the trembling
of weather and drawn-out daylight.

Words will not be able to bear the weight
of your discoveries if you will love me a little longer.
I can be a parable in June.
In June, I can run faster than the dark.

Neutrinos

In the late afternoon, I walked out
to where the highway begins and thought
about regret. How it will not die
and endures beyond everything:
beyond tenderness, beyond the wisest,
darkest deceits; even beyond
the next loving time under a blanket.
I raised my hand, shielded my eyes from
the sun--red in the air--watched cars
going by too fast to learn a thing
about them. That is a law of Physics:
*Things go by too fast to learn anything
about them.* Here's another one:
Nothing comes to those who ask.

In the house, I read about particles
from 150 thousand light
years away. They are so small, they pass
through the earth without touching any
thing. 900 trillion miles, pieces of stars
coming from an abyss, going to
an abyss. We are not protected
by our songs or our dances or our dreams
when heaven's minutiae can enter
and leave us with no sign at all.

Neutrinos . . . *continued*

We might be in a dance with smoke
and mirrors; me in the kitchen
reading of novas and neutrinos;
you, stroking your beard and going
over the possibilities. You're
the Piano Man, I'm your Buck and Wing Gal.
We tap in our patent shoes, out to where
the highway begins, and try to recall
the Act Of Contrition without
remembering why we need to say it.
If we shower each other with rue
and reminiscence, a poem may come
of this, after all. It will be
a love poem, I think, and will pass
through you, touching nothing.
You probably won't feel a thing.

Lost Causes

When I asked to buy a school
sweater, Mother laughed out loud.
"We are poor" she said, "poor as
grape pickers, poor as buttons,
poor as pretzels!" She sat stiff
at the sewing machine, her back
a bent rod, her foot moving
up and down on the treadle.
Sure, she was nuts -- crazy
to death --but mother could SEW.
I slept warm under her quilts;
my father ushered at church
in suits she invented, then
tailored, our furniture was
covered in Mother's patterned
episodes. My faded father,
seldom spoke on my behalf,
but offered the observation
that she certainly couldn't
sew a sweater. She looked up then,
winked, said "Who says I can't"?
The sweater lost to me, I left
the room muttering, *Anyway, buttons
aren't 'poor'."* She told
me to keep a civil tongue
in my head which I have done
ever since.

Another Cinco De Mayo
... And I Still Don't Know What I'm Celebrating

If you were writing in Greece, your face
would be burnt just from the glare off
the paper, the sun off the paper.
Unless of course, you decided to write
on the rocks jutting out of the bay.
At that point in your life you might find
some comfort in the stories the beach
children tell: of how a very rich
woman came there with her dog --
an expensive, pedigreed something--
and had to be hospitalized for
an island kind of dysentery
brought on by the eating of too much
feta and the dog strayed from the hotel
kennels and now lives, eating scraps,
in the winding alleys of the island.
Or, how a frail young woman from the Bronx
saved for six years to make a trip
to Greece and lost her money -- yes cash--
on a boat excursion and, having
no family to cable her fare
to get back, she moved into a small
white house, moved in with an abalone
fisherman who cannot even pronounce
her name. She pronounces his just fine.

Another Cinco De Mayo . . . *continued*

Or about the red-bearded man who
came from Chicago after killing
his wife by serving to her tainted
crab meat which he used in his famous
Newberg sauce. No one is certain
whether the woman's death was an
accident or not (or even worthy
of note). But, he lives on the island now
with three lovely girls who are all good
friends and happy to share him amongst
themselves. If you were writing in Greece,
the scalding sun might turn this into
a love poem and you might end up
writing it for some engineer
who cannot even speak Greek
and does not remember your name.

Go Away, I'm Cleaning

A movie an old one with James Stewart. Doesn't matter what movie but the scenes were of San Francisco in the 50's. In the middle of the movie the cars, the fashions, the buildings, the storefronts seemed so old and I had to turn it off because it's oldness pressed down on my chest like a thousand pigeons sitting there and I didn't want the movie to be about some time in the 50's I wanted NOW and only NOW with no oldness around to give me nightmares. So then my hands got cold and there were great gulps of sadness in my throat and I couldn't turn the damn thing off. I had to watch it all the way through until my heart broke and made a mess on the living room floor and I had to clean it up. After that, things were better.

Supernatural Episodes

I think we have to keep our supernatural episodes down to a minimum, what with a war to win and all that.   Col. Korn in Catch 22

It has dawned on me that I have said
Too many things about the deceased.
I never intended this, but it's
what happened. I write about Life

and still the dead creep in from all corners
of the room; huge and without
hesitation, they climb over me
as if climbing over granite hills.

None of them are unknown to me.
Every day I profit from their
histories and their laughter, their secrets
which they told me:

 Mother, as she sat at her sewing machine, told me the details of her abortion-

Daddy explaining that he was actually born in Hungary and came to the States when he was two. This was a fact that embarrassed him-

My cousin's pregnancy and immediate marriage; her decisions to turn her back on shame then rule the world-

Supernatural Episodes . . . *continued*

My hero poet Larry Kramer telling me that he'd be walking
through the fire into some other world, telling me that I would
have to write my poems, finish them without his imprimatur.

My sanguine friend, M, whose smoky, Jersey-kissed voice told me
over the phone that she had 6 months to live. She lived three.

This planet has its rules. You can bury
or burn the dead, but, in the quiet
times, they will stare at you wordlessly
until you wise up and let them in.

Local Color

At the lake,
the swans nearly
levitated. They
moved so smoothly, like cells
splitting and joining at the
beginning of the world. Beauty!
I tossed bread and they ate-looked grateful,
floated-silk winged, breathless. But when I turned
to tear more bread, one stepped ashore, tottered toward
me, bit the back of my leg. It left a mark that
looks like a closed eye and has never disappeared so
that I carry a reminder of beauty's ingratitude-beauty's greed.

And Back Again

I am divided: North, that stand of white pines;
South, the clean pond;
East and in the evening, the brown bats;
West, the rusted farm things. All this
will be here long after I have told you
each detail. So, if I give you this scene
more than once, love me with patience--
know that some dreams will not be still.

With The Koi . . . *For My Father, John J. Reisz*

In the long afternoons
I sometimes dream of you, Dad,

so tall--a child's lie--rattling
the pages of your newspaper.

Your glasses glint, your eyes
strain white, then I wake.

You did not know, that morning,
how the students were cleaning

the Koi pond and found
at the bottom what looked like

a human hand. They walked down
with buckets and brushes

and fine clean intentions to drain
the Koi pond and scrub its sides.

That's when they found it; just after
the pond was drained, the Koi afraid.

In the evening, the nurse called
to say, *"Hurry, your father*

is dying." And I began
to move like Esther Williams

With The Koi ... *continued*

in a water ballet, like
a Piscean ballerina--

selfish and keen and beautiful
in my reluctance. One student

laughed; another, they say
vomited, but the one

who fished it out,
a tiny Vietnamese girl

studying Civil Engineering,
only pursed her lips and sniffed

and suggested they get on with it.
I'm grateful, Dad, that you were not Catholic;

had a priest been there, I swear,
I would have cried to offer him

the usual thing. Instead,
I touched your dry hand, stood

a while to harbor. . .something
for your emptied self.

A Certain Relief

Though I love rain, love to wake up in the night
hearing it-hard at the windows-there is
a certain relief when it's over, something
below my level of physical
awareness, a certain comfort knowing
that daylight will show a familiar dirty
landscape. The air will stay clean for just so long;
the streets will shine, proffer reflected stars
for only so many nights before the grime
of acid clouds spreads itself again over
this city.   Rain or not, in the late afternoon
I will eat at the small table in the alcove
as if dreaming, saying, "O I see: here,
under faces, is language. Here, under
language, is the sound inside the words."
And, though I love rain…I don't know anymore…
I guess you need one hell of a strong belief
in the Devil in order to understand fear.

Aftershock

Before time came and went and made me afraid
of its comings and goings (mostly its

goings), I knew things about ponds and prayers,
and fields too and moons and the deities

prior to Jesus. I was a revolution
with no regrets; the Sandanistas would

have loved me. There was a story I held
in my sleep: the manuscript neatly typed,

no errors, the famine on my doorstep.
First the noise, then the quake, then the quiet.

Knock knock. Who's there
Justin
Justin Who
Justin time

Only now are they able to report
the data-the seismographic figures.

"Women Buy Clothes As A Form Of Prayer To A God Never Satisfied By Offered Flesh"
for Marge Piercy

Mark Strand, poet of some standing, says,
"Most poets dry up at 50." Hell, Mark,
I'm 62 and I can't even lose 10 pounds
much less dry up. But it is, after all,
the thought that counts. Thanks anyway.

from

After The Earthquake

Xlibris Press ~ 2007

Salutations And Prostrations

Glossary of Names
Shakpana-Destructive God of Dahomey
Mythology
Abbadon-Hebrew Archangel of Armageddon
Nenaunir-African God of Storms
Shigidi-A Yoruba deified nightmare

A black wind desaturates our once-
colorful land. Now our homeland quakes
in gray and white images.
Soldiers again,
missiles again.
Black blood flows over our sickened land.
You can hear the rush and tink of it
in your ears. See it at the back of your eyes.

President Shakpana-Pox Bringer–
give us back our children!
Secretary of Defense Abbadon-Angel of Hell-
give us back our husbands and lovers and wives!
Secretary of State Nanaunir-Rainbow Snake-
give us back our mouths to say against you!
Attorney General Of Justice, Shigidi-God of Hate,
master Torturer-
give us back our animal radiance.

A black wind whips our skirts, hair, scarves, trees.
We parody smiling at you from
our noir deserts. We don't have the courage
to be unruly.
How can we overcome
what we are not permitted to see?

Salutations And Prostrations . . . *continued*

Touch me, hear me, world on fire,
world drowning, world with windows closed.
Turn up the damn radio and send
this out-this fucking rage, this fucking
lack of respect, this fucking-our just fucking.

Eshu, do not undo me,
Do not falsify the words of my mouth
Do not misguide the movements of my feet.
You who translate yesterday's words
Into novel utterances,
Do not undo me.*

A black wind desaturates our once-
colorful land. Now our homeland quakes
in gray and white images. How to valorize this…
Now we are all third world-everyone born common
is third world-and this spiritual blackmail
Makes it late afternoon no matter what time
Of day it is.

* a Yoruba Prayer

Fall Air Tastes Like Whiskey

It's a little darker
a little earlier
in the day which always
makes me sad, so that, if
I decide to take a
walk to the corner
Mercado to buy club
soda or a lettuce,
I come home a bit drunk.

Maybe I miss Summer's
exploding sun and the
drying milkweed on lawns
across the county. Maybe
it's that passage from the
scent of cool gin and tonic
to the slightly metallic
gold-brown of whiskey.
It just makes me sad, that's all.

This whole "time passing" thing
leaves a lot to be desired.
My mind and the damn mirror
never agree and the
argument is getting
pretty old. Summer is
leaving. My star is going
with it. The green stalks outside
are neon tubes, the sidewalks

Fall Air Tastes Like Whiskey . . . *continued*

are hard again. I always
forget that part-the damn
sidewalks-cool, hard again-
not rippling in the heat
like some dream you want to
talk about but don't. When
I drank, I'd see September
in with a small snifter
of Old Bushmills Irish.

But, hard liquor makes my
head hurt now, so I have
to welcome the season in
whining and sipping tea,
and seeing the planet
through clear, painful eyes
instead of victoriously
clinking ice cubes and tasting
Fall's blood spill on my tongue.

Awakenings

> *You'd think at a certain point, all these a-typical somethings, would amount to a typical something, but a typical what?*
> **The character Dr. Malcolm Sayer**
> as played by Robin Williams in the movie "Awakenings."

These words, in front of you, will
open the door to a brand
new insanity that will
thunder inside you, give you
a blessing. You don't know it
now, but, by the end of these
sentences, you will fear the
things you desire:

strong drink,
  long hair,
    banging doors,
      purpose,
        company.

After you read these words, you
will relive the pain-basting
you got when a lover left
you for a wealthy woman.
(Late that night at the bar, the
barkeep said, "Baby, it's always
about money." You muttered
I ain't your Baby, fuckhead,

Awakenings . . . *continued*

and ordered another Old
Bushmills.) These words will remind
you of poisons and dancing
and dope which is why you won't
buy my damn book. Who wants to
remember the second-best
sex they ever had or their
weird Uncle Toby's ceaseless

whistling or getting knocked on
their ass in the old
neighborhood which is a stone's
throw from the one we're in? These
words will make you weep, these words
in front of you now. They will
send you searching for a sleeve
on which to wipe your nose.

They will force you to take an ice
cold shower, scream, masturbate,
kill spiders, but-worst of all-
they will jumpstart your memory,
make you scurry to reclaim
territory long lost in
the hunger and sleep that is
your life.

Until Dark
for Saul Landau

I see through the open window,
the trees are trying to avoid the gray sky.
To their embarrassment, there's no getting away from it.

Those trees are in it until dark when everything will relax.
Until then, they must whisper to each other
as conspirators will do from separate phone booths.

My friend weeps at night. It is the way he relaxes in the dark-
crying over the lost revolutions and the lost soldiers and the lost
farmers and the lost families.

My friend has declared an allegiance to humanity that upsets the
governments-present and past. He is apt to vomit at hearing too
much foolishness.

His anger is hypnotic, but he waits for dark to weep. Who has
been dragged off to prison, he wonders; who has been beaten until
dead; how many junkies can dance on the head of a needle?

He knows that everything built in the desert soon becomes sand-
another reason he weeps.

> Blessed are those who give away kind words. Blessed are
> those who do not take academia seriously.

> Blessed are those who know that Hitler and Nixon and Al
> Fatah live in the bathrooms of their neighbors' houses (and
> they still hold back their tears until dark).

Until Dark . . . *continued*

Cry for the CIA,
cry for the prisoners,
cry for the DEA and the police-secret and public,
cry for the gang lords and children of the gang lords,
cry for Korea and Vietnam and Iraq and Palestine and Chile.
Cry because Castro is getting old,
because buying has replaced learning,
because it's the last drink and the bar's closing is so fucking final.

> Blessed are you, friend, writing letters to those who have forgotten how to read, pleading for Nirvana to find the young and for Transcendence to embrace the old.

> In a dream, I saw you slog through Chiapas to get to Xbalba, then returned and wept.

The sky is gray and tired. It recognizes you, understands that, whether it offers ink or water, you will swallow the world.

Several Years After Your Death
   for Patrick

The pale stripes of light
across the grass
move, change shape.
The gold sun slips down
until all color-inside and outside-
is defeated, brought to its knees.
My sighs, the dark shape
of the footstool and the palm fronds at
the window-it all freezes,
as if shock visited suddenly and
paralyzed the world.
Buried under years of *whatnot*,
My body cradles the thought
of you. Outside-under
the lawn, small lives
grip the dirt. They move,
they live, they refuse to emerge.

Epistle To The Romans

For we know that the whole creation has been groaning together in the pains of childbirth until now. ~ Romans 8

When we think back on it, we'll call it "the end times" and remember the strongmen tying knots in their thick ropes just before they used them to bind up the bulls and drag them down.

We'll remember how false confessions were forced out of the mouths of our daughters. The infidels used poisons and magic to effect this - a worthy pursuit for witches.

When the sea pulls out and out further, getting ready for the enormous tidal wave, we'll think of the bears and the chimpanzees-how they were released from the zoos and were then free to roam what was left of the earth.

(I don't remember what happened to the rest of the animals, do you?) The sea will pull out, as I've said. You must believe it or you'll have no part in the dialogues. We will call it "end times,"

and reminisce about seeing bats-how they followed the seagulls out to sea and drowned there (as did our Nana's only son. She had daughters, but poor, drowned Ned was her only boy.) We were raised on mysticism and mine disasters

and we watched our fathers spit tobacco out into the orchards or the fields or the ocean. We will look back at the last of the sunflowers leaning so low, and we'll recall the "end times," swooning at the way the brown sky infiltrated houses,

Epistle To The Romans . . . *continued*

and temples and concert halls. The proper incantation is the one that brings loved ones back to life after they've passed over to the other side. My mother knew this, so did her eldest sister. They held hands sometimes

and chanted it low and sweet over the newly-dug graves in old cemeteries. Now my mother has died and my Aunt, her eldest sister, says there are no incantations. By the time the grasses have all been burnt,

and we're all afraid of sex, as we used to be, the only good books will be photo albums with pictures of the "end times" as we remember them. While the hookers count their stretch marks and the pimps count their money,

we will chuckle over the way hundreds of cars simply stopped on bridges and people got out of the cars and looked over the sides down into the lakes and dry creek beds to see if anything could be devined there.

We'll call them "the end times," and nod solemnly. We will cut our eyes to the side and smile at each other's chatter; each of us will believe that he or she owns the truth. Not so. We all know the same secret:

there is sunlight and there is snow and horse piss steams in both. The "end times" will buckle and roll in our memories. Hoping for further mercies, we'll walk naked to the sea; we'll stand and watch it disappear.

Rapture II

We've had this discussion before.
The catechism you recite strikes at me:
> "Jesus Christ is coming! Are you ready?"
> Nobody's ready, friend. Poor Christ
> wouldn't know what hit him if he
> ventured into our impounded souls.

Sure, we keep praying for way out and roads in and strength and good luck.

But, it is not Jesus we seek.
We seek domination, we seek right with might.
> We keep turning each other's pages looking
> for serpents in the gardens. We discard the obvious
> and engulf ourselves in layers of artistic turpitude.

We no longer vibrate with the desire to speak free, BE free.
We can't live with what we know is about to happen so we withdraw.
> Snails are braver-they go forth, from their shells,
> to get somewhere even if it means suicide.
> We keep a nodding acquaintance with Jesus.
> We pillow talk with Jesus,
> (with Buddha, with Allah, with Shiva),

but we sleep with guns in our hands and genuflect in bombed out temples
on uniformed knees. Friend, we've had this discussion before:
> Jesus was clay the same as Judas; the same
> as Gandhi; the same as you. In the end, we cover
> our faces and tremble while repeating "It wasn't my fault"
> to whomever is left to listen.

Health Plan

Suppose this: A man thinks
his heart is on fire with love
for a very thin and beautiful
woman he met at the Las
Palabras Bar on Olive St.
Then he learns he has
bronchitis and that it wasn't
his heart at all but this
infection of the lungs.
He is very disappointed,
but my guess is his mother
already told him these things.

Symptoms

Where to start…?

Let's say you wish it would rain when you know it
won't for a long long time?

No, begin here:

Maybe last night, you died and this morning they
found you and everyone cried except the landlord
and you see yourself, being presented to
the hospital authorities in a black
bag because you put it in writing that you
wanted to donate everything-all your bits
and pieces-and the hospital morgue guy bows
humbly to your spouse and thanks him. You wonder
if you should have gone the other way and planned
a funeral.

Begin here:

the landscape is an army of dark scratches against
a tarnished silver sky. Some water is dripping
from the clouds, a little at a time. A hand
breaks through the window of a deli to steal
a wheel of cheese and shouts are heard. Some people
run toward the scene. A woman turns toward the shouts,
loses control of her car and crashes into
a light pole. The cheese was made of plastic-
a display.

Symptoms . . . *continued*

Here is my last hint:

A woman looks at a picture of the moon
and the sea. She looks at it for 3 hours, then
notices that she can hear the waves crashing
in the picture, can feel a mist. She pays close
attention. Soon, it's time to pick up her niece
from ballet lessons. She turns to leave-a man
walks up to the picture, jumps through the frame.
He drowns. She is late retrieving her niece.
What law could possibly apply in this case?
You can't touch without being touched-
Newton's Third Law
Where to end…?

End with the way a chair takes your shape, holds it
after you've gone off to bed.

End with the purity of a white pillowcase-
how quickly it becomes limp, used.

End with the last bird on the last day of September;
how it answers all sighs and oaths, answers thunder
by bathing in a puddle on the balcony.

Here. End it here.

Fourteen Miles Outside The Cape Of The Poor Clares, A Name I Invented
Pfeiffer-Big Sur August 19, 1984

The hugeness in this silence is a net;
it hauls me in; a dream after too much drinking.
Everything here moves, swells, is excited,
quelled and dropped, to be picked up again
and far flung around rock points. Like a
convalescing tubercular, cautious
with my steps, with where I sit, what I eat,
how I move. There is hope for a wind
redemption, but it is long in coming
as are all healings. These white-wrapped seditious
visions are impatient, need an instrument
as I need instincts-mine are worn. I make
a fist, try to force a way into my
own stillness. Breaking and entering, stealing
what I will not give. Two with me here:
two aunts; one alive, to do me an
unkindness, one dead, touching my face while
I sleep. We had not seen each other for weeks,
then she died I was abased by that then
and am now. This is not about the death
of an aunt, after all. It is about
the ocean and the quiet river and
wood smoke filtering through the valley at Big Sur.

Letter To An Old Friend

I want to try to explain this right.
The way we sat together there in your room,

different music coming from behind all
the doors up and down the hallway.   See, I

was there trying to save my soul
which was not what workshop fees cover, but

the truth is that I already knew how
to do what I paid to learn how to do:

write and make love and watch from corners.
You were there for all the right reasons: to drink,

and hear difficult things and teach quiet ways.
Each night, I fell asleep with the music on,

waiting for something to come through the window
and save me. (Mosquitoes do not count

for this purpose.) My dreams then were open
slashes, bleeding and bleeding until I

weakened and woke up before it was light.
everyone thought I rose early to write,

but the truth is that I sat on the bed and
hugged my knees and thought about making love

Letter To An Old Friend . . . *continued*

to someone every day and night for the rest
of my natural life–to a man or

maybe a woman whose skin would flush
at my touch, or the sound of my voice.

It would not have bothered you a bit to
hear that confession; don't care now, I'll bet.

O Lizbeth, I am 62 years old,
and I remember you leaving me in

Vermont and how I stared and stared at
your car driving off down the road, dust

kicking up like in the movies. Later, at
the motel, I said to the dial tone, "Come

save me, Lizbeth, or I'll probably die." You
had hung up a long time before and

I still remember how the telephone looked
with your voice all over it and the odd
things my hands were doing to each other.

Sparrow Hawk Season

There is something very likeable
in the idea of the sandy
ocean foundation-the way it shifts
until one place is not itself
anymore at all. There are infant
forms beneath the water: you and I
particularly are virtuosi,
rehearsing love as we would lieder;
blending, faces raised in unnatural
harmony. The horizon harbors little-
a "brightness" that "falls from the air."
You there, listening in on this,
scarcely moving lest I notice you…
You there…what are your dreams?
To be a bird of prey? To be several,
or only one, or forbidden?
I have sat for hours here-twisting my hair
through my fingers, watching the light escape
across the desk, irretrievable as a sleepless night.

Sparrow Hawk Season . . . *continued*

If somehow, there is a sense of dusk light
about me, know that I have always been
like this: crippled and cauterized
by patience-rage in plaits down my back.
sleepwalking, my only exercise-
the diary, my only recourse.
I am this…and this…
all of my lies are leaving. They will
abandon me-all my lovely lies-
packing their gear and tiptoeing off
into a crenellated somewhere.
fugitive lies, (sulking, slouching away)
without decision: an act of famine
as certain as time,
more fragile than fear

Drinking Wine Right From The Bottle

If you believe Christ will come to you,
that he will stumble and grasp your ankle
to break his fall-
you are all matter and
no meaning.

If you believe that evil echoes
like stiletto heels on tile floors
and that it shakes your shoulder repeatedly
to get your attention, you may find that
the best solution is to live somewhere
other than Earth.

Find a place
where the creeks run
with the exotic blood of mythic birds
where the leaves laugh, and you are your own eyes,
and dragons are mistaken for bridges.

The Angry Affirmative

Don't gloat. You were just my moment in the woods,
a smudge along the clear edges of my self.
I was attracted by the lust you had for
the pain of others and by the hint of un-
spent energy behind your eyes. I told you
that you were beautiful-that was prattle, leaves
rattling in a windstorm. When I joined you in
your bed, stained your sheets, it was, I admit,
coercive-what could we do for each other?
I regret nothing between us. You thought, "She
will remember this always and I will not."
But, I can tell you now: as you stretched yourself
over me-a scar that ran the length of my
body-I remember very little. There was dark,
the lack of room in your bed, Ginsberg's words:
Businessmen are serious, movie producers
are serious. Everybody's serious but me.

The Big Couch

I just want a normal life with roast beef and swiss cheese and a big couch"
(**patient speaking to HBO crew** in the documentary "Bellevue")

Wonderful the way
everything simply
blew up all over
the world. We were bored.
Coke didn't excite us;
Pepsi even less;
reality T.V.
smelled like decayed fish;
microwave popcorn
was making our stomachs
hurt and none of us
were ever going
to meet Paris Hilton.
Then God smiled. The war
in Iraq heated
up real good; Hurricane
Katrina leveled
the South; a little
girl was kidnapped and
killed; there were shootings
in several bad parts
of several towns in
several states; the war
heated up some more
in Iraq; the strange,
handsome hero/villain
on General
Hospital went nuts.

The Big Couch . . . *continued*

God chuckled and gave
us the gift of watching
Enron flinch, watching
catatonia take
over the film
industry, watching
the wee beauty queens
wink and prance and
seduce the salivating
pedophiles gazing
and blinking at them.

Wonderful how it
all blew apart.
Now we were excited.
Now we waved our hands
wildly pointed our
fingers, shouted.
"The world is blowing
up," we yelled, "run for
your life!' It was good;
tasted good with chips and beer.

The Full Moon Rises

Everywhere I look, someone is screaming.
I've gotten quite used to it now. I used
to say, "Calm down. All will be well," but now I
just let them go at it.

The woman in the green skirt is screaming
because the birds won't come eat the bread
she's tossed to them.

The girl in the yellow sweater is screaming because she waited
up all night for her husband who picked out someone
from a bar and went to a motel with that person.

The man with freckled knees who wears
the dark blue shorts is screaming because his lover
seems more remote than a sci-fi story and won't say why.

The boy in the sandals is screaming because he did too much
"Baby T" on Saturday night and, when he woke on Monday,
he was alone in a gas station bathroom with his dick caught in his
pants zipper.

Everywhere, someone screams.
Like bats,
like lobsters,
like penitents,
like owls,
like burned skin,
like a line of Marys-
all of them Mothers of Jesus.

The Full Moon Rises . . . *continued*

In that sickly hour between light and dark, there is the screaming
of a Summer lost. At the door of an office,
there is the screaming of shadows and paradigms.

Though nothing I say can introduce you to real wickedness,
the screaming of the seven deadly sins will
give you more truth than your heart can hold.

Everywhere I look, someone is screaming.
I am quite used to it now, but I think it is only
fair to warn you:

There is a new knife cutting the night,
my brother, my sister.
There is a new shimmer on the water.
Bare your throats and listen for the screaming.

from

Hunger

Xlibris Press ~ 2007

All That Jazz

The new Jazz Age
> reeks of dissatisfaction,
> avoids aging,
> fears death,
> gathers useless tools and useful friends,
> invests on the margin,
> plays golf,
> contributes to the Red Cross,
> drinks raspberry vodka,
> toasts the Cossacks and the Beatles,
> spills expensive perfume on the neighbor's duvet,
> mutilates bodies,
> swirls Cabernet in a stemmed glass,
> separates conjoined twins,
> devours women,
> exhales men,
> is ravenous

and too full to notice.

Planning A Covenient Future

It has made us all crazy:
war after war until it is all we think about and
the only thing we do not
reveal to one another. Our insanity, brought on
and brought out by the damn death
strokes we want to forget. When we speak
on the phone, we are sure to
have music playing or the TV going so as to
mimic harmony. How did
I learn to hate war so when my entire life has been spent
listening to its statistics,
watching its consequences? I've been sold grits and Drano
and Halloween candy in the
midst of war's hallucinations. I learned the role that "cool"
must play in putting one foot in front of the other,
planning a convenient future,
imagining a God who manages to ignore the
need for bravery. So far,
I've felt no obligation to shoulder any blame in
these pissing contests, maybe
because I am a woman and have not known women to
love war as many men do.
Damn death and its saccharine
messages blurted out on billboards across this pained land!
Damn the way we've been asked
to wring laughter out of Korea's tears, Viet Nam's sweat,
Iraq's blood. Yesterday at
the grocery store, a young woman and I exchanged comments
about a can of Irish
oatmeal. She says the can has the colors of a bullet.

Planning A Covenient Future . . . *continued*

She says her husband, in Baghdad,
sent a bullet home as a souvenir for the son he
may never see again.
O city of god! How many of us are there can dance
on the head of your pin? Feet
too large, hands too large, hearts too large to wrestle angels for
that space. This song rises from
a locked throat. I wear dark clothes so that you will not see the
stains of my patience bleeding out.
This is the singing of snakes in an unforgiving opera.

What We Did

Too old to blush, but I did, said
        I'm not sure how to please you-I want
(I couldn't look at you)
        to please you
and you said
        come here
and stretched a long white arm to me
and I took one step only.
        My husband
I said
        writes down his disappointment in me.
        He writes it in a brown journal
        he bought from the bookstore .
You said
        your husband is not here
and stretched the other arm out to me.
        Take off your tee shirt
you said
        or let me
and I took one more step to you and looked up
and you laughed-very white teeth invited me-so
I sat on the edge of the bed.
        I don't know what to do to please you

What We Did . . . *continued*

I said
        and I want so much to please you; I'll take off
        my tee shirt.
That stupid scar
under my first rib
glowed like nuclear
waste. You tongued it,
asked
        Your husband?
        Yes.
I said.

Your breath on
my shoulder came close
to being a threat
it was that wild, that
ragged. Your fingers,
lit from the inside,
tattooed wherever
they touched. Your mouth
created graffiti
on my back. You breath
stroked clear through me,
kissed me so long, so hard,
my lips tasted like
bruised apricots.
        You keep your eyes open
I said
        You look at me while we feel or stroke

What We Did . . . *continued*

You said
        Only the blind don't see what they touch.
I smelled the pear blossom
outside your window
and we had some wine
and your dark hair
quieted my hand.
While you were inside me,
I imagined you
tying off my veins
And filling me from
a syringe full of
warm mists. Languorous,
unable to open
my eyes, pinned to you,
I knew exactly
what to do to please you.

Before The Fall

There has been too much written
about it: the loneliness
of a sky-bright evening,
the stars a little broken,
walks not taken for lack of time
and other dull things.

This is some kind of strange love poem.
It didn't start out that way…
the California air propped
up on damp ocean stilts has
maneuvered these words into
a frame of loving, quiet

as an empty pillow.
It's better not to think of it.
O, there are still the traces
of summer: afternoons too hot,
a lethargy, more light than
we'll have in November.

Before The Fall . . . *continued*

But, summer's rudeness is gone
and, in its place, there is
courteous, crisp weather
and a kind of arrogance
to go along with it.
In the fall, people don't

approach me in the hallways
to tell me jokes like they do
in summer–not that I'd laugh
if they did. It's all too sad;
Fall is very nearly here
and you, my love, are not.

Call Waiting

Some days, the only things that make sense are
sleep and hot coffee
and maybe a scary movie
to show you how lucky you really are
because no hose-nose zombie monster is trying to hack you into bits and
eat your face off like in the movie.
You really are lucky because no slimy swamp thing is holding
your ankle with his talons while you scream and try to get out of the water.
And it is pure luck that none of this is happening to you personally
(although the brunette who is chained to the table saw and is about
to lose her head to the blade resembles you a little).
Some days, the only sensible thing to do is sleep most of the day
to keep yourself from stewing over your most recent diet
and the overdrawn charges in your bank account.
When you wake up, you'll still have your head,
no one will have eaten you,
you won't have drowned
and you can heat up your coffee.
Of course, by that time, it's 4o'clock PM-
7 PM in New York
and your fucking agent never did call.

Insomnia

If you *sleep* (well not actually sleep)
with the well-known writers,

you hope their luck will rub off (or flow into) you.
You know you aren't ever going to be part

of what Bukowski calls their "Circle Jerk,"
but maybe you could screw your way

to a good word-maybe a review sometime
in the *Los Angeles Times* or *Poets & Writers Magazine*,

or a vote of confidence in an important poetry competition.
Seems like the least they could do, after you give your permission

for them to sign your dance card,
is come up with some kind of artistic payoff.

All I know is I gave it my best shot, but gave up, finally,
trying to screw my way to the middle.

The sex was mediocre-they don't fuck like they write,
they don't buy presents,

they don't compliment your new outfits,
and they refuse to discuss your work once you've done the deed.

Insomnia . . . *continued*

Well, you'll do what you want,
but I'll tell you this:

one of the best shaggings I ever had
was with an overweight housepainter

who bought me a beer and a hamburger and,
the next week, painted my kitchen for free.

Your Mother Weeps In The Mezzanine

What is there to sacrifice now?
    An MP3 Player.
    A computer game.
    A bottle of wine.
    A fat Polish Sausage cooked on the grill?

God must want something you are capable of giving up.
    The flames in your eyes as you watch
        a child's polyester hajib melt into her skin is not
enough.
    The choke and sob of one citizen alone in the TomKat
Theater
        on Santa Monica Blvd on a Tuesday afternoon is
not enough.

Give your curses to God; the stars can eat your hatred and shower it back down on you with a vengeance.
Your face turns the color of a sunset while you finish the sequence:
    Love,
     Faith,
      Commencement,
       Commitment,
        Betrayal,
         Anger,
          and the final exhalation.
Then the movie is over.

Your Mother Weeps In The Mezzanine . . . *continued*

Your mother weeps in the mezzanine. She whispers "Splendor, splendor"
or something very like it. Her grief is fathomless.
You could sacrifice that-your mother's failures and her tears.

Maybe you are not a believer.
Maybe you think no sacrifice is required.
The day you refuse to sacrifice, the sun will not rise,
> the sea will quietly drain into sand and become desert,
> the Eiffel Tower will melt into the city streets.

You must find the right offering. You must take it to the warm chemical tides of the Atlantic and deposit it there.
I know-this is a lonely responsibility, but everything depends on you.
It just does.

Intention

I want you to squirm inside this poem.
>I want you to know how black your passions can be.
>The tingling you feel when you consider caressing the ass of your exceedingly beautiful brother or sister or both if you have both-
>that tingling is supposed to be reserved for anyone BUT relatives.
>Yet, there you sit, hoping to conceal that which will remain unsaid.

We've made a vocation of refusal:
. our darkest wishes for how to end loneliness stay hidden.
. the images of what we would do to be warm stay hidden.
. the sharp gray thorns that do not quench our sexual thirst stay hidden.
. the needle used between the toes to sate our appetites stays hidden
. our laughter breaks off like icicles from a tree branch, falls-falls-falls and
   lands with no sound-even that cold silence is hidden.

I won't point out war-how we live it, fuel it, make love to it.

The laws governing our trespasses are not clear.
>We stand in shock at our blindness.
>We stand in shock at our leanings toward desperation.
>Underneath sleep, we move on all fours toward streets
>>gone red in the sunrise.

I am not explaining evil to you as I know it.
>(Come in, sit and listen.)

I am introducing you to your own violence, you see.
There is nothing beyond that.
We've all bitten off more than we can chew.

Glass

It was just a mirror,
> dreaming it was a mirror.

It called itself by some name it heard
> and didn't dare to say.

As children, we looked into it, saw it looking back,
> hungry for our faces, our soft little hands,
> grimy little hands that opened and closed,
> our small teeth ready for anything.

We glittered and beamed
> and dreaded the after-supper dark.

I have dreamed it too many times:
> the television reflected in the lift-top mirror;
> the clothes dryer that rang out "How Dry I am"
> after each load of clothes was finished;
> the monsignor come over for dinner.

Just mirrors. Each dream is only that-
> a mirror believing itself to be more-
> perhaps a chandelier on the Titanic.

I dream our faces lost in cigarette smoke,
> drenched in the belief that we
> and all who knew us were immortal
> (hence the interest in Vampires and
> Werewolves).

My sister's boyfriend was so intent on seeing her
> that he tore his hand vaulting over the chain link fence.

Just mirrors. Dreams are only that-
> mirrors thinking they are prophecies
> or fairy tales.

Glass . . . *continued*

Our family was clearly at war.
       My mother picked shards of glass
       from out of the bible and scattered them
       like seeds across the carpet.
She watered the floor,
       encouraging them to grow into mirrors-
       some round like wreaths, some like hexagons.
       They bent in the mad wind that blew through our house.
The glass seeds that refused to grow
       lay glittering in the carpet,
       waiting for three sisters to step on them,
       track blood all the way to the kitchen table.

Black Velvet

A new religion that'll bring you to your knees, black velvet if you please
song lyric by Anthony Vita

We all noticed it at the same time
--a tic
--a tremor
--a slip of the tongue

We saw it in each other before we noticed it in ourselves

--a weakness in the knees
--a bruising of the heart
--a slight burning sensation in the eyes.

Soon we came out of our houses and apartments and double-wide trailers. We heard it then

--voices shaking
--groaning and clearing in throats nearly closed with grief
--disfigurements and breakdowns in the soul

Train whistles went mad, there was no reason for anything. Some of us were drunk. Some simply went foolish, stuttered, shot heroin.

Warheads were shuttled around underneath us, down near hell. They named them: Pluto, Mars, Charon, Ares, Thor; and the full bodyweight of consciousness
was in them.

We knew then what we have now forgotten: our lives are a combination of unlit hallways and traces of sweat. God is aware of the recently resurrected madness.

Black Velvet . . . *continued*

He hears the cries for compassion coming up from the sinkholes and brambles. I don't know how long he can love this world or how long any of us can. We have been taken so far from what is true that dirt no longer sticks to our shoes.

So, what to do? Marilyn Hacker, that delicious poet, says we are *too fat, too smart, too loud, too shy, too old, unloved and underpaid.* I like that, it addresses my tunnel vision.

So what to do? Joni Mitchell, that delicious poet, says *With a good dog and some trees out of touch with the breakdown of this century They're not going to fix it up too easy*

So, what to do? Paul Thomas Anderson, that delicious poet, says *It all comes down to what we can forgive.*

Forgiveness is as contagious as confession and smells like old clothes.
I don't know what I can forgive.
I haven't tried it much.

Well, It may be that there is nothing to do. Perhaps I will have to find my own way. Perhaps I will have to end this poem and let you decide what it means.

"Ghosts Seem Harder To Please Than We Are…"
Elizabeth Bowen

I am aware of the way the dead come back to us—
they visit in rivers,
in rooms,
at tables
and desks,
in corners of dreams,
in fevers,
in quarrels,
in the humidity of sex.

My dead nuns, tall and unhappy, rarely visit.
We were less than kind to each other when they lived;
it is certain they have less to say to me now. My grandfather
liked me quite a lot and laughs from the inside of rivers.

The steam rests over the miso soup from the Thai restaurant next door
and my friend Marianne visits in that steam. We often ate together.
Her death was sudden and I prefer her miso-steam visits
to the dreams I have in which she is no longer my friend.

The monsignor who came to watch football with my uncle visits me
during arguments with my children or a bus driver.
The monsignor's face, a mask of pale, stiff wrinkles, cautions me
to stay quiet, remain seen not heard. He makes the sign of the cross
on my forehead and vanishes.

"Ghosts Seem Harder To Please Than We Are…" . . . *continued*

The old Polaks who sat around My Aunt's kitchen table,
lean into their *kielbasas* and *pierogis*. They eat loudly,
smack their Slavic lips and turn to me, wanting to know
what will happen now. They are long dead. Their smiles
are insinuations into the light sleep leading to dawn.

The dead do not look forward to visiting us.
They so rarely make it clear what they want
to give or take from us. If they're interested in sex,
they squeeze themselves between bodies and rest
there, relishing the way One + One = One.

Knowing this, I still look for them in the places I've mentioned.
I have promised my own loved ones that, if I should drop in on them
after my demise, I will call them by name and explain at length
what I want and why I want it.

Gin And Tonic In Charlotte

We take the night sky far too seriously.
We stare up at it as if there was nothing
but time to do so. We give the white winks
in black depths such power, blame lost love, love gained,
fate-all, all centered on stars-white and winking
in secret dark.

And then the moon! Good God, the moon!

It's alive, it's dead
It governs tides,
It has a face
It is cold/warm/huge/small/near/far/has been conquered/has never
been truly visited.
Its blankness, when full, causes madness, good sex,
unconsciousness,

and, I believe, a desire to share our pasts
over iced drinks on a porch swing. We have made
the night sky a stern parental presence who
will punish our indiscretions with round, pale
yellow light and rashes of white twinks that could
easily fall and prick us like nettles.
We need a new set of parents. They must be
kinder than angry bees and clever enough
to know when to ignore us. We need parents
whose love for us is not endless or pure or
unconditional, parents who will get over
us in time, unlike the night sky which remains
a thing we take much too seriously

Enhancement And A Red Moon

I think I have been dreaming-or recalling a dream-
something about a razor and a rosary.

I woke up as the moon kissed the last of black night
from my mouth. The moon licked at my wrists and fingers

and woke me. I am a transplant, a refugee,
as we all are. Aren't we detained here, not knowing-

in that "Kafkaesque" way-why? The martyrs tell us that
the dice are loaded and the flames of the crucible

burn-unending, without mercy. I believe it.
Getting warmed up is my métier and I believe

every martyr I've ever heard speak. There is no
such thing as timeless. The chewed and torn cuticles

of passing hours are people I have come to know
in the way the pious know the stories of Saints' lives.

Do you know God? At dusk when
the sun sets, God comes out

from the indented rocks to hear prayers, to feel warm guilt
flow over his feet. At dusk, the bees go to sleep

and cannot welcome him. They're filled with a holy
urgency, but are helpless, too cold to move.

February 20, 2006

The world changes, we do not, there lies the irony that finally kills us.
The character **Armand** from the film <u>Interview With A Vampire</u>

My birthday today-I am 62 years old and have swallowed
whole the words of my sisters' lives. I have seen them
make their way toward unthinkable horizons, to their beginnings.

Today I am thinking over all my own humbug and my magic tricks,
none of which have tidied up the rubble in my life. How can
a heart remain whole when it remembers everything?

How long did it take for me to learn that love could draw
a knife across my throat as easily as hatred or fear could do it?
I don't remember. It took a long time.

When did I finally know that not listening was a kind of death
or what it meant to be lied to?   An acquaintance asked me,
What does it feel like to be in your sixties? What a question!

For a moment, my whole dumb life stuck in my throat like
an unchewed piece of red meat. I was overcome with a
clouded passion for all I don't know-don't care to know.

    (Whisper to self: *So, what **does** it feel like?*

   Like I am a veteran of the local color here.
   Like I am looking for a freeway to take me around
  the side roads.
   Like I have been ravaged by what might happen.

February 20, 2006 . . . continued

>*Like I am lewd, screwed, and tattooed.*
>*Like I can't figure out how to live outside the betrayal of my body.*
>*Like I have learned to arrive on schedule like the trains in Italy finally did.*
>
>*Like I no longer have to stomach the foul atmosphere of rage.*
>*Like I no longer have to practice a look of scorn, confidence or cool*
>>*in the mirror to get it just right.*
>
>>*Like it will all turn out fine, with everyone learning something*
>>*from this experience; with the music rising up in the background*
>>*and each of us looking meaningfully into the camera.)*

Patriot

Only the truly Wicked understand dispossession.
They know how to keep life at the wrong end of binoculars.
It's a belief system: they praise Adam for being free of sin

until Eve entered the equation. They ignore the provincial patterns,
seeing themselves as too quick to die.
They believe they can outrun death.
Ha! They've consumed too many fortune cookies, believed the

messages inside. I have nothing against the Wicked-nothing at all.
I've loved a few of them, been in bed with one or two.
There's nothing wrong with them that a humiliatingly
personal relationship wouldn't cure.

I have no curses for the Wicked. I've cut my teeth on them. They
opened my doors of perception like huge gusts of wind. They lie
with me In the fearful early-morning moments when my demons
twist, whisper. *Maybe the phone will ring; maybe a*

*neighbor will shriek, maybe we'll all go certifiably mad before
sunrise.* Only the truly Wicked understand about these maybes.
They'd like to scrape *maybe* off their shoes, then go about their
business having barely made a ripple in the space-time continuum.

In those 3 a.m. moments we all fear, the defense of the Wicked
comes easily to me: I tell myself that a great sadness makes them
Wicked,. A lack of bonding with their mamas from the beginning
is the cause of their wickedness. Being roused

Patriot . . . *continued*

uncermoniously from a good nap once too often has taken them
off the good-guy track, made them desire the carnage they leave
when they consummate their desires.
Ah! but nothing I write will introduce you to the Wicked.

If you have paid attention to this poem, your life now
has more truth than you can handle. You're in way over your head.
Just by reading, you've become part of my plot
to instruct and improve America.

Today an apostolic rendering is all I will own up to. I might own
up to a five-year longing I once had for a dark-haired
rock and roller with a head for computers and hands for me.
But, you don't need to know all of that.

Your interest lies in the demise of those things, not their ability
to skirt the limits of the living. You want to know
if I've pulled away from being perfect,
if there is any hope for you to do the same.

Ah, my finders, keepers, dreamers, weepers! The reflections of
our mothers stand behind all of us.
They reneged on their promises and will unstitch us
on our way to heaven-birthday by birthday.

Bi-Visiblet

A fly-fishing term describing a fly with both light and dark colored hackles to give good visibility in both light and shaded water.

Amazing the way we are still not
embarrassed over the proliferation
of Barbie dolls!! We're not actually

embarrassed about the proliferation
of starvation and great rolling machines
with iron underbellies either. We

are truly repelled by poverty and
the insistent wordiness of the aging,
but we've not yet reached overload on

personalized license plates expertly
painted by elves in orange jumpsuits. The days
are often made of small, incomplete deaths

which we try to ignore-their intimacy
too humiliating to contemplate.
Visions of some high school boy

who'd had enough of being not enough,
pass through our minds while we stand
like croquet stakes in line at the grocery,

thoughts too, of an apocalypse
in the far east, holding hostage the prayers
we can't find time to say. The umbilical

Bi-Visiblet . . . *continued*

cord that connects us to the Almighty
is a one-way feeding tube and America,
my dear fat girl, doesn't do the feeding.

In the parking lot, we push our carts in
this direction and that direction, holding
our car keys like rosary beads, heads swiveling,

chanting, "Where is it? Where is it?" Our first
lives here are not so much failed as foolish.
We march around in yellow waders and

cast our rods without skill, watching the river
riffle and return empty hooks. "Where is it?"
is our first-life mantra. We have not learned

compassion yet. Our hearts pump only enough
blood to remind us of dinner time and
who not to make angry. We live in an

endless silence broken by gull shrieks and
giggling, None of us is sure what to do
about the sudden finish. Imperfect

German cursing drowning out imperfect
English, swearing, and the momentous blast
bringing destruction to our embarrassing

Bi-Visiblet . . . *continued*

memories and our too-little-too-late
helpless humanity. We will know
dimming street lights and

trains slowing to a complete
stop and will hear the beautiful voices
of our own children calling out to us

as the children in the far far East call
for their parents. In our most turbulent
discussions, we never imagined-

never dreamed, never believed that our
ugly dying selves could be so crippled
so confused.

That Which Separates Us From Lentils
A Love Poem

I dreamed
        inside
                the new bedspread
                and
                there was beer and envy in my dream;
                it was too scary to share-

suffice it
        to say
                I was glad the
                2 AM pee call woke me.
                Then you woke as well,
                then came back to bed, then
                stroked my hair with a warm hand.

I hoped I smelled good,
        then
                hoped for
                more stroking.

Our 21-year love
        is palpable
                in and out of bed or company;
                one + one = one we say-
                and sleep curled together
                like furred animals.

That Which Separates Us From Lentils . . . *continued*

This world offers me
      nothing
            save time with you.
            Someone should paint you
            bent over your maps and web pages.
            Someone should
            count you as one of California's
            state treasures.

I count you as
      my drug of choice.
            Our sanguinity is flawless.
            We combine skin and spirit
            and sheets.

I dreamed
      we were in a movie
            titled WHIMSY. When I woke,
            the sky was gray-white,
            demanding to be let in,
            demanding to be included.

Sonata For Three Violins And A Kazoo
... With Signs Following

I hate ukuleles. I'm not crazy about
accordions either. Confronting the familiar
just isn't my bag. Pry any of us open
and what you'll see is the Self as an empty lot,
an abandoned mine, a dry well, an empty bag.
Pry any of us open and you will find
something bright and unspeakable but essential.

Hasn't everyone had that dream of flying over
blue roofs that flow under their feet like little
oceans. That is not a "special" dream. We've all dreamed it
or something like it. Let me persuade you that, despite
your lofty ambitions, you've only learned to live
your own impairments and you've not begun to touch mine.
Something keeps us from facing the tough questions. I think

It's too much dessert after dinner that does that-
the fear of belching out the truth over Fudge Cake.
The tough questions**:** If I don't reply to you, did you say anything?
What if *The Rapture* is nothing more than the cessation of our own
mediocrity?
Called upon to create a moment of cataclysm, could you do it?
Are your thoughts better digested if washed down with Old
Bushmills over ice?
Do you really want revenge?

We learn to turn our faces from ourselves-lovers
invent us, create us from the curled pages of
our own burned books. Granted sight, we say , "Glad to see you"
and "Haven't seen you in a while" and "See you later."
Still we are blind.   The trio begins tuning up.
The man with the Kazoo steps up to the microphone.
The signs follow.

100 Select Poems *plus* one ~ Martina Reisz Newberry

from

Perhaps You Could Breathe For Me

Xlibris Press ~ 2009

Requests

I've done some begging in my time. Sometimes,
          if I wanted something or didn't want
something very much, I'd run my mouth like
          a Singer Sewing Machine. I've begged from
God and from men and most often felt men's
          response-God may have been busy watching
love's milk flow onto the belly of an altar boy.
          A man on the bus told me,
"Think back to all you've begged for and see if
          any of it was worthwhile." That is what
prompted me to think about this. I know
          that the more I've begged, the deafer God and
men became. I don't know the reason for it,
          only that it's true. When I begged for the
painful moments to pass quickly, they went
          on forever. When I begged for moments
of paradise to stay with me, they were
          off quicker than one stanza of Row Row
Row Your Boat. When I begged for foi gras, I
          got bologna; begging for lunchmeat got
me crab cakes and Old Bushmills.
          Another, wiser person might be
discouraged by these results, but not I.
          I stay on top of the begging process,
knowing that it can cover vast places,
          new territories and, in the end,
will be its own reward.

Study Of Trees

When I think
of you,
I think of
that Japanese Maple
you showed
me in a
magazine,
such dark green,
it felt like black.

Stronger,
more beautiful
than anyone
I'd known
before you.
I think of you
and your soft hair
and your poems
(as if my mind could settle

on anything more beautiful
or more sad).
I remember telling
our mutual friend
that you bedded
me as if it was
your last time
ever, as if it was
with your last breath,

Study of Trees . . . *continued*

as if fucking me
answered
enough of your questions
to provoke the rest
of your life.
What I felt
for you
was a prelude
to the rest of mine.

After you left
(and years after that),
I hated
the world I knew
before you.
I hated its lack
of the gentle
thrust and flow
you taught me.

After I left
(and to this day)
I loved the world
you gave me.
Loved its
recklessness,
it's angles
put at ease
with passion.

In The Kitchen

It is the start of November.
The plumbing has stopped up,
the plumber is on the roof.
We have waited all week for him.
Who knows what the pipes' sinuses hold?

It's my fault.
I was a neglectful daughter
A mediocre mother
and a lapsed Catholic.
This is what happens when you fail.

60 - Something Female Poet Writing To Her Country In The First Decade Of A New Millennium

Can you please start passion's engine again so we can climb aboard? Can you invite even those with motion sickness? They will come if invited, heads over the side, gaily puking trepidation, happy to be included.

Will you let us revisit desire, view it in all its incarnations: as an ache in the skeleton, as contemptuous recognition, as weakness, as madness, as religion, as disease? It still blossoms inside us, regardless of cosmetics' effectiveness.

I understand the bias. I see the stuff that lives in people's eyes and throats when they look at me and compare the numbers. (Thinking of this, I lie awake, especially on those nights when the moon-a great jaundiced eye-

hangs on a silver chain, stirring my chest's heat, stirring its dust. In the mirror, my deranged haircut looks out at me. I am drawn out of and back into myself.
I accept the image, but not the implication.)

If I speak persuasively on behalf of us all, will you crave us? Will you embrace our thin-skinned bodies, dedicate yourselves to allowing us our beauty?
We can still be ignited. We can still burn.

Praise

Say prayers where it is dark, unfathomed, unworthy.
    Whisper them in a quiet, desperate voice
    as if-instead of God-you were talking
    to a scientifically-tuned stranger.
Say the prayer of the gap-toothed man
    who touched the stripper's shoe, knowing-if caught-
    the bouncer would have him shaking blood from his hair
    like a dog emerging from a lake.
In any case, that would be the prayer to say. It will not,
    cannot keep you from dying,
    but may give you enough time
    to stop cringing, perhaps change direction,
change the color of your body, learn to give off some kind of light
    the way animals do,
    the way birds do when they check
    under each wing then
praise, full-voiced, their ability to fly through the great skies.

Philosophy

The bald man at the reading told me
"You're not particularly
Existential are you?"
I stuttered, I guess not.
But the truth is I am. I do
all the things the other Existentialists do:
I write, slip on icy sidewalks, get lost on
the freeway, watch porno movies,
spill mustard on my blouses,
sit in bird shit on park benches, bang my
head on cupboard doors, burn my tongue on hot
soup, weep into the space where wind blows through.
Maybe he couldn't see it, but I'm as
Existential as the next guy.

4 P.M.

I thought today might just be the day
    of *never again.*
I never again wanted to pay
    Respects to a bad
Mammogram or stutter my way through
    a conversation
about chemotherapy, baldness,
    rebirth or stained sheets.
I made it to 5 pm when a
    brief note from an aunt
announced the death of her daughter, my
    favorite cousin,
in a skiing accident, she said.
    It may as well have
Been a murder for all the difference
    "accident" made and
my efforts at saying something precious
    in a return note
ended up untidy and polite.
    I sent it anyway,
with a great show of purpose. I took
    it to a nearby
post box though it was raining and cold.
    Nothing now to think of
except that *never again* is only
    on loan to us and
is as unfaithful as fragrance,
    as fire, as a face
lost in a starling's dead eye.

Beautiful

Beautiful isn't it,
the way some beaches are sand
and some are small, smooth rocks and
Beautiful
the way the water bends like molten silver
when the weather is hot and
it's late in the afternoon?
Beautiful
the way the sky tears down the middle
for lightning and mends again later on
Beautiful
how breath turns white in the cold and
how the world's roads move across the land
no matter what
Beautiful, isn't it,
the way love rhymes with glove and
silk rhymes with milk and
rage rhymes with cage?
Beautiful
the way the light stays on and on
during the Summer months and
a different kind of
Beautiful
when Fall makes it fade early
Beautiful
the cleanliness of bones in moonlight
when the desert is silent and without wind

Beautiful . . . *continued*

Beautiful
the cool rind of a honeydew melon
and the perfume inside it inviting taste
Beautiful,
the way a woman hums to herself
while she gets dressed and
sighs one hundred sighs
when she undresses
Beautiful
the accident of passion,
the brush of hands, then mouths,
then bodies doing more than brushing-
flesh on flesh
to music older than the stars

Beautiful,
the smell of soap
and burning wood
and frying onion
and a diner far up the road
that you didn't know was there
Beautiful, isn't it,
the smooth red bark
of the manzanita plant and
a long teardrop earring
that touches a woman's neck
and how Beautiful
a full cupboard
jars of delicious things

Beautiful . . . *continued*

There is the Beautiful
ice sculpture
with perfect pink shrimp surrounding
and the Beauty of buttered potatoes
Beautiful the strange trailing roots
of water lilies and
the zippers on dark leather jackets
Beautiful
the figurine
of the two-headed saint and
the red satin lining
of the box it came in

Beautiful
a new book, a new shirt,
new sheets, a new pen.
Beautiful
the lover that used to matter,
the one that matters now,
and the ones that never mattered
Beautiful
a pain that stops,
a cut that heals,
a scar that was earned,
not inflicted
Did I say how Beautiful
Is the purity of a
man's shaved head
or the long, dark hair,
a man might have—like
a river down his back

Beautiful . . . *continued*

Beautiful
a drinking glass so clean
it looks like water
holding itself
Beautiful,
a runner, a cyclist,
Kabballah,
birthday cake

Beautiful,
the way you read
or hear this poem—
your eyes wishing
for everything,
wanting this to be one thing
that will not be content,
one thing
that will not be captured.

Ashes

I regret my savage empathy for all the
wrong things. I cut my hair short because I was
exhausted from tearing it out, from twisting it
into knots, from setting it on fire and running
for my life.

I live with a waxing moon that takes the place of
rational decision making. My neighborhood
is one of flesh and remembering. These days, my
body rejects the wild run of Irish whiskey
(refuted love is what they call that.

Symptoms? Migraine, nausea, double vision and
overwhelming sadness-all this at first sip). Where
I stand, it is very still. The umbrage of the
colorless sky goes unreported

but not unnoticed. "Look here, the sky tells me, "if
Icarus couldn't touch me, no one can." So, I
reset my goals as I have so many times, clear
away the broken glass,

sprinkle a little cinnamon on the window
sill to discourage the ants and lie down-free of
guilt, breathing into the glare of an open blind-
ready to dream of paradise.

Postures

I had a friend who said this:
"The only thing that you can

count on is loss." I never
quite bought that. I've counted on

other things:
The uncontrolled appetite of Guilt

the disarray of Wisdom
the long thirsty threads of Desire

the short streets of Love
the blank stare of Dark

the longing in Summer Solstice.
I've counted on all those things.

I've counted on the urgency of Light,
the music of the Purple Bamboo,

the tug of fingers braiding hair
or the way the smallest pond of water

doubles the beauty or the
ugliness of anything.

You can count on the way
we go at sex like ferrets

Postures . . . *continued*

put on capes and pray
to fly off buildings insuring

the safety of the entire population,
who will remain eternally grateful.

You can count on all of us to continue
grasping and gnawing on each other,

watching to see who gets the best morsels,
snarling with love and strangled by our prayers.

Ah well! I hear the questions you want to ask
You think this may be a kind of curse on my memory,

delivered by one of the unforgiving deities.
If it is a curse, it's a damned useful one. It forces

my perpendicular mind to run parallel races.
You can count on this: it's either loss or

a culmination of all our fantasies.
Whichever it is, I am tired of contemplating it.

Better, I believe, to study the calendar,
study the clock, study God's Labyrinth,

and afterward, tell my raggedy stories to those
struggling to stand upright in a tilting world.

The Looming Whatever

The looming Whatever that
waits for all of us-the un
doing, the resistance,
the way we push against the
sun and the violent
forever of October
is unsettling. Tiny bird
beaks of regret go poke-poking
at our hearts and we weep.
We weep and tear at our sleeves
and try to be reborn in
a Jesus whose dance card is full.
Remnants, chalky faces at
the windows of heaven,
bloody knuckles at the door
to hell-all this is planned for us.
When it's finally evening,
we serve denial with
Chicken Marengo and Hemlock
with a Marzipan Truffle.
We lie down with Whitman and
get up with Good Morning
America. No matter
the words or the music, no
matter the seduction of
memory, we remain
indefinable; we use
up the inside minutes
of our bodies. I write all
this down-first one way, then the
other-
using words as stick figures
to proclaim each death a new death,
each rebirth a little less palatable than the last.

The Hang Of Happiness

Fall again

and old fears return with
winds that tear through the canyons-
old battering rams-insistent,
beckoning fire.

San Jacinto mountains,
San Gabriel mountains,
San Bernardino mountains,
Tehachapi mountain range

Fall colors here come from real fire.
The trees explode with heat; they tremble,
smoke, blow to bits, turn to sparks that scatter-
a kind of pollination as aggressive as any other.

I can't think of poems in this atmosphere.
Essence of Self is all that floats on the smoky air:
Why here? Why now? Why ever?
Ash and fire push at the sky to welcome Autumn.

The small gray birds get themselves down
the mountains and into town to share the sidewalks
with the rest of us. The slower ones stay,
die and drop from the trees, eyes bright as sparklers.

The Hang Of Happiness . . . *continued*

The old fears:
Is my pen too heavy? Is my heart?
Each Fall, fire obscures the road
and I can't find my way.
I lose the hang of happiness.

But, I've learned to cultivate a patience
(born of knowing)
to fill my parched white days.
The road to salvation runs

directly through all the seasons,
whether I like it or not.
My life will be repaired at first rain.
I'll enter happiness with the expectation to stay.

For Real

Reality is wrong. Dreams are for real.—Tupac Shakur

I dreamed
of Tenderness,
that poor cripple,
dragging herself
down an empty road.
Bereft of saints,
but happy to be
anywhere at all,
she limped along,
gathering
the loose ends
of souls
and smiling
a hungry sliver of a smile.

Boulevard
    for Brian

On the bus, I heard a guy say into his cell phone,
"I got a Love Jones for ya…" Oh Baby, this is the
way it is all up and down Hollywood Boulevard.
A Love Jones-yeah! I'm sugar-doughnut happy over you,
blood-red rose happy, Jumpin'-Jack-Flash happy. We're twenty-
one years together and I am right here on this sidewalk
wanting one of your gap-toothed kisses like it was the
very first time ever. The sun quivers all over us,
signals dance. My bones make bell sounds, my seasoned limbs
shout "smart," shout "brave," shout "real." Your mouth says
"beautiful" and I hear "always". I'm all over
the map with you, Baby-South to Sunset, West to
Santa Monica, somewhere between yes and no.
I am a hip-hop lady on crack-crack being love
and crack being crazy, crack being pink-lipstick nuts for you.
Your hungry tiger smile makes my toes curl upward and
I can't keep from cupping my hands under your chin
to catch the sun. I'm whiter than bleached flour,
but I know about Love Jones: we're twenty-one years together
and I still want to abdicate everything to be in your arms.

The Ugly Building On A Hot Day

On the bus, I met a man who said he'd killed his wife.
He said he'd done it sure as shit and would I like to
see her body. He said, if I went with him, he'd show
me her body. It was July and hotter than I
can describe, but I wanted to see that dead body,
so we got off the bus and I walked with him past cars,
and railroad tracks and garbage and old drugstores and
empty lots. We walked a long way until we got to
a square apartment building painted ugly green and
festooned with graffiti. Oh loyal readers, I know
what you're thinking. You wonder why I'd want to see
such a thing. You can't imagine the horror of a
dead body in an ugly building on a hot day.
Listen, there's more.
We went up two flights of stairs, he tapped
on door number 312 and walked in. A woman whose
blue apron matched her eyes jumped a foot in
the air when we came in. "Dear God Clark, you scared me!
Her apron eyes came 'round to me. "Dear God Clark,
not another one. What did he tell you, Honey? That
he killed me and wanted to show you the body?"
I was speechless. She put a hand to her forehead.
"Dear God Clark, what next?" I wondered that too.

Bad Manners

I don't know who to be angry with anymore.
That's a lie.
I do know
but my rage can't find a release tunnel-
something or somewhere to race through.
I need to see someone with real power
apply a tourniquet to the hemorrhaging
of the mortally wounded countries my country has stabbed.

It is not enough to see the burning bodies on the news in High
Definition;
you must know that our backyard barbeques mask
the smell of smoke across the planet. It is not enough to know
that in my country there are mothers in jail for protesting the
deaths
of their children who were forced to kill other children in other
countries-
children who were told to kill them.

Knowing is nothing
Fury is nothing.

Oh sweet America, I don't crave forgiveness for not singing
"I Love Barney" songs
with your babies when I know that the scent of Khinta and the taste
of Khubaz have been stripped away from the noses and mouths of
those you help to destroy.
I'm not some remorseful woman in a shopping mall unable to
grasp the notion of what belongs to who. WE belong to WE.

Bad Manners . . . *continued*

The windows through which we watch the world are cleaner than
our hands and the ghosts fleeing by those windows no longer care
what languages they speak.
Talking of how the water of the rivers in Liberia became beds of
gravel, and the hills of Sarajevo were too gouged and flattened for
snow play, a poet said to me "All you can do is write it again and
again until honor turns some of this around."

There's a chance he was right and there's a chance that it's bullshit
and can't be turned around. So, here is that place in the poem
where my rage and futility
has made me teary and tired.

Listen please.
It is not indigestion keeping you awake nights
or the thoughts of a heart you broke
in some fit of bad manners or microwaved lust.

No, this insomnia you suffer is made of oil and blood blending.
This insomnia is the total absence of Love as humans have known
it.
This is unabashed Knowing climbing into bed with you,
putting its hands around your throat and squeezing
until your heart bursts open and its pieces
scatter over the world like petals.

from

Late Night Radio

Dog Ear Press ~ 2010

Unidentified Flying Objects

Ageless in the dark,
a young woman is enthralled

by the paranormal
as if it was next to her in bed.

She longs for a ghost story of her own,
some strange thing to mull over

in her insomniac hours. The radio says, "They're coming for all of us in the dark.

They'll come in their silver cylinders, their silver suits. Their huge black eyes will

stare through us." Ageless in the dark,
she hollows out a space in her heart

for these great-eyed creatures. They are far from sleep as she is, intrigued by dark

as she is, foreign as she is and still they are untroubled. She is not. The radio

ups it's own volume. "In just a minute you'll hear
the sounds of an actual UFO

landing and the cries of those watching it."
She waits through a commercial and

another and still another,
waiting for sounds she'll never hear.

Lucid Dreaming

Observe the people around you and repeat these words:
"Everybody here has dreams."
From Lucid Dreams in 30 Days by K. Harary,Ph.D and P. Weintraub.

When the weather is good, my *chi* warms to it. Kindness is born, old grudges are forgotten, I resent nothing-not even my years. Today, I re-visit a dream: a huge house, too many people, noise, my breasts bare and the inability to find clothes.

When the weather is good, my dreams bloom like flowers in a certain season, die the next day unless I write them down. Those of us who expire in our sleep, die of what are called "natural causes." Those of us who wake after our sleep are called "frightened."

When the weather is good, reality soaks into my diligently plowed fields. I worship all tenderness, all hope. I dream nourishment and gliding bodies. The air sings with my fullness. Only sleep remains when all of this is through.

The Number Of The Beast
British Petroleum Oil Spill Disaster, April 20, 2010

"A vast amount of oil one mile beneath the surface has bled since April 20 into the Gulf of Mexico. According to BP, it's about 200,000 gallons a day; researchers at Florida State University estimated about two weeks ago it was at least 1 million gallons a day, and even more recently engineers from Purdue University predicted it's probably closer to 2.5 million gallons a day." ~
Dr. Reese Halter, *Conservation Scientist*

The heart bleeds best. In waves, in miniaturized tsunamis. It is "goodbye" that does it or strangling sobs licking away at neighborly veins, kisses that are unrelenting, unreturned can do it. The heart bleeds out in 6/6 time-a perverted waltz-rhythm death-more often than other accidents. Pain, pressure and a huge sadness and the accident begins.

The ominous plumes of oil venting from this pipe...one mile beneath the surface - are behaving unlike any other oil spill ever observed before. ~
Dr. Reese Halter

Ebola virus frequently twists itself into a shape that looks like a "6". Six letters in "genome," did you know? When a person becomes infected with Ebola the virus multiplies and, after six days,

Ebola symptoms can begin. Again, it's a blood game. Swelling, seizures, more swelling until finally human pipes burst and blood, columns of it, pushes up and out onto the open sea that was body.

As they worked on the system underwater, the effect of the...spill was widely seen. Swimmers ...rushed out the water after wading into the mess. Brown pelicans coated in chocolate syrup-like oil flailed and struggled in the surf.... The oil on the beaches was stained in hues of rust and crimson, much like the color of drying blood ~
Greg Bluestein, Journalist

The Number of the Beast . . . *continued*

Call it collapse. Call it cruelty. Call it heartbreak and lost love and regret. It's all the same and sweet Sister Earth knows it. Should we remember ORPHA666? Glass Bone Disease. A "bulge" in the collagen complex, whites of the eyes turned gray, bones shattering, *Long live Ivar the Boneless* cried the crowd. Six letters in "malady." Six letters in "genetic." Six letters in "cystic."

Thank goodness the White House has approved five sand berms for Louisiana. The berms will be paid for by British Petroleum. There will be a total of 6 sand berms to protect Louisiana. That is positive news I suppose. ~ Kate James, Gather News

Mr. Sandman,
bring me a berm*,
make it a strong one,
hearty and firm.
Please turn on
your magic worm.
Mr., Sandman bring me a berm.

It is written that,
if you have reason-
understanding-
you can recognize
the Number of the
Beast
because It's the
number
of a human being
and a human being's
number is
Six hundred threescore
and six.

Berm = Fortification

Lost Civilizations: Chernobyl, April 1986

*Without question, the accident at Chernobyl was the result
of a fatal combination of ignorance and complacency.*
    Richard Rhodes, author of "Arsenals of Folly"

At night, the moon rides the wind.
Trees whose leaves die some each day
are afraid, bruised and baffled

at their own mortality,
still growing from poisoned soil,
untouchable soil. What few

stars there are blow around the
Exclusion Zone and through the
broken glass of The Rainbow Shop

which is littered with the crumbs
of children's toys. The glowing
Ferris Wheel and the irrational

skeletons of bumper cars
hiss and creak, never doubting
that their time will come, never

doubting their memories of
an opening day. Why can't
it be real? We've always known

that reality is a
matter of choice. Even in
Prypiat-even there-we

Lost Civilizations . . . *continued*

seize what we want to believe.
After a while, the tale takes
on its own shape so that we

can tell it to friends at parties.
The broken glass, a doll's head,
a poster still clinging to

the wall-it's all true, it happened.
The word "accident' makes a
fetish of the lies that let

us move forward while we look
backward. That word, "**tragedy**"
will turn each of us to salt.

Conspiracies, It Might Be Best Not To Listen

This poetry,
straight out of the anguish of my own mind,
is not for the strong.
I'm just your average Los Angeles lunatic,
looking through the veil of tourists
for family.
I used to write for the beautiful and courageous, for the models and the film stars.
But that
was a long time ago. Now, I write these poems
for the scarred and the fragile,
the slapped around, the twisted up, the homely and the harassed.
I can't be poet for the mighty. Circumstances change.
The stars crackle.
The sky takes on light-pale yellow paint on a porous ceiling. Each monstrous event of a life
is more monstrous
than the one before it. It becomes better for you
to tell yourself the most terrifying stories
rather than have me tell them to you.

Chakra - Ajna (Brow)

I know what a third eye is supposed to be,
but that doesn't make me want one. First of all,
it's asymmetrical. Second, it's always
looking for the truth. It shows my erosion
and the shambles I've made of things. I don't want my blockades
dissolved in wisdom's acid rain. Buddha wants me to stop
scavenging and start thinking with my spine. A third eye would help me do that,
but I would rather not partake.
I picture the white faces of some Charolais
cattle, then alter the vision by placing a third eye above their noses. It's dreadful.
They become monsters which is
what happens when any living creature wises up.

Wicca - The Ovaries Of War

Since being given the gift of suicide-
eons ago-from Adam (God's first-born, God's favorite),
we've not needed reasons to go on living.
We are giant kites: paper, sticks, string-
matter looking for structure, looking
for music to dance to. We make our love-spell
dreams into poisoned tea, send our lovers off
to battle, mourn the passing of those who pass
the cup to us. Heaven is made of I-told-
you-so's and irreversible confessions
forced from us by angels with sabers.
Once we disclose our hearts,
we are released and captive at the same time.

Remote Viewing

Candied neon flickers, stays,
flickers again. The streets are
black-slicked and everyone is
inside dreaming that the day
will pass without incident,
will bring an evening
without incident. Someone
asks a question. Someone
circumvents the answer.
The rain outside calls for waiting.
Maybe until morning when
everything will be clearer.

Druids

The trees are trying
to come in again-
that time, that season…

All year, they know their
places, don't make a
move on us, but, when

April hits, they reach
for the places they've
been eyeballing. They

cheerlead the wind-green
pompoms shuddering,
waving-until it

touches down on our
patio. Slim green
fingers crook at our

timid tomato
plants. "Change places?" they
ask. The trees want to

change places with our
struggling tomatoes.
They envy our old

Druids . . . *continued*

bistro set and the
coffee-and-incense
smell coming from in

side our apartment.
"Change places?" they ask.
Green beards on old-man

brown faces. They wink,
they grin, they reach, they
whisper, "This world, this

world made of words and
gestures, will see us
in. Make time, make way."

The Fate Of Consciousness

All those days,
all that weather with pain in it
and nothing
passing through our town-not even a freight train-
all those days,
so quiet, filled with birds and bombs you could see
but not hear.
It all seemed unbearable somehow,
with a little terror around the edges to liven things up.
My thoughts shudder
when I allow them entrance to my inner nature like that. Not two
weeks ago, I climbed a dirt path
to try and shake lemons from their branches.
The thorns surprised me and I thought
of all those lost days,
the sky full of arrogance,
the sun's shards reluctant to pierce the sky.
(Why, I'll never know.)
My memory of it is profound: cloistered kisses,
fever blowing in to strip the bark off the trees,
settling for good in the open mouths of our tulips.
All the lost minutiae of that other life-
the decision to live or die in it…

The Existence Of The Ten Realms Of Being

Pay attention. Better to know exactly
what "elsewhere" means
lest you be alone when the rituals
are recited.

Even your name is not your own
unless you chose it. Our comforts
can only backtrack, coax us into the past
where it seems easier to live.

One long exhale and our wings are attached,
gears shifted, cloth cut cleanly
by the inevitable razors
handed to us by belief.

Pay attention. The skies devour us
the way our secrets do.
We are seldom intact, our bits swirling clockwise
then counter clockwise, flying off into the trees,
then further into the bluescreen evening.

Pay attention to our rearrangements.
They are eternal. Here, a tree-
a Japanese Maple, here a lizard,
skittering on sand. There, a park bench

or maybe a slim, lithe-bodied girl
with hair as long as a promise. We're mysteries
even to ourselves, jealously guarding
the desires we must learn to live without.

Channeling

The rules of this board game are tough.
They require the knowledge
that that my voice will be
among the voices you listen to.

and your acceptance that you'll never
see innocence again. This will be easy to accomplish.
My voice is simply that of a snail
who dreams she is a painter,

a painter who dreams he is an electrician,
an electrician who dreams he is a horse,
a horse who dreams she is you and, finally,
you who no longer dreams,

who only cries out for a name that denies forgetting.
I can't be your channel
or your stone or your saint.
Once, in a time of hope, I sang you,
magnified your face in the glass of my memory.

I watched your doomed wits as they were passed around—canapés
on your mother's finest china. The voices are there. What spirits
there are, morph into verbena flowers when I try to tell their
history.

Channeling . . . *continued*

I channel poorly, yes?
I look and sound too much like myself
but it seems to suit you.
Am I the Talmud you protect?

Am I the tome of Ruth and Naomi's love for each other?
I understand: you can't believe that all we're meant to do
is to become voices coming from someone else's mouth,
and you're right.

There's so much more.
We were born from rivers that rush
through this earth on their way to a covenant.
We flow in all directions:

creating, mimicking, cutting through,
and claiming all as our own.
Our story is about standing still,
   hearing   listening   paying attention.

100 Select Poems *plus* one ~ Martina Reisz Newberry

from

What We Can't Forgive

Infinity Publishing ~ 2011

Collateral Damage

First, there was a thousand years of famine,
then a moment of surplus. Death's flawless
dreams waited for our silent coming. We

bloomed-black Narcissus on a bruised and
desecrated desert. We set the clocks
for the earth to explode under us.

We ignored the signs, transfused the wounded
with tainted blood and gave medicines that
dissolved the bones of our brothers. We cut

open our sisters' bodies and placed bitter
leaves in their wombs. We polished our own hearts
with aluminum salts borrowed from the

cellars of devils. We delivered fears
and fevers and the certainty of God's
malicious ending. Where death lay sleeping,

we woke death up to sort our morals from
our memories. We, the conquerors of
cracked earth and merciless yellow sky, moved

on without apology and death stayed
behind, where we left it. *All this, all this,*
we cried, *we did for Peace.*

"... I Feel Myself A Cog In Somethin' Turning."
Woodstock—Joni Mitchell

I was a goddess before you were born.
It was I who kept chaos at bay,
kept the serpent from eating you whole.
Naked, fearless, I tracked him to his tree
and, though he thought it was his scheme,
I seduced him and pulled the apple
off the fruit-heavy, generous branch.
You retreated to the darkness of
a cave and, when the new voice thundered
"Where are you?" it was I who stepped out,
squinting at the light, licking apple
juice from my fingers and palms. Oh yes.
Contrary to popular belief,
it was I who stepped forward proudly.
"Here I am," I said, "You wanna piece
of me?" The new voice, angry, and thick
with lust, answered, "Hell yes! Here I come!"

What Madness Is

Madness is anger's placenta,
a thorny cord that strangles,
a finger that writes "no more" in death's fluids.

Madness is this confession: *I have encountered my enemy.*
I wanted to set fire to my enemy. I wanted to perform
unnatural acts on my enemy.

Madness is a dream in the morning-of transitory waters
and the ruby blood of *I love you* moving between
the tired legs of a tired woman.

Madness is that white mania that leaps from stony heart
to stony heart, turns the universal mysteries into
fishhooks and phantasms.

Straight out of the black sea comes the madness of Amen,
the madness of allure, of sex that cripples your senses
(it is that vigorous).

Madness is the tight knot of wisdom and hatred
and, later, ecstasy of a kind
known only to the saints.

Anarchic and unassuming, madness brings
a coward's blades to the throats
of the world's inquisitors.

Madness is no vindication. No escape plan.
Only these words, clenching inside you
like fists, like teeth, like closed eyes.

A Thousand Signs

I have been naked in soul and body
with women whose names escape me. I have

shared my body's portfolio with men
whose hearts were too heated to resonate

anything but a divine urgency.
It makes me wonder: is love a sickbed?

Can we love ourselves only if we see
our lust for others as disease? I am

drawn to an impossible point of light,
a sign outside my national language.

I am free to read it. I am free to
view the wreckage of a thousand signs in

a thousand places. I have seen the light:
men who love men are splotches of sunlight

in the shadows that cross the deck. Women
who love women are rivers of questions

on a desert planet. The rest of us
tremble, intend to be happy, take love

A Thousand Signs . . . contrinued

back from the bold ones who have sheltered it.
In the end, we are all caught, made to walk

the gangplank. In the end, every night is
All Hallow's Eve. The gilded sky covers

all of us and, regardless of choices,
We all take it hard when we die

Unraveling The Day

The night is alive beyond
the blinds closed against it. In
bed, my eyes speak: "Sleep" they say,
"and don't see what isn't there.
"Whatever you do," they say,
"don't look back at today." But,
I do. Hell! There isn't a
woman born who wouldn't look
back at her near-done-with life
going up in flash and smoke.
It's the death kiss, after all,
that we're waiting for. If that
final glance backwards turns us
to salt, *she'y'h'ye**. The death
grip of the blinds in this room,
the death kiss that follows; these
are what we wait for.

*So be it

Untitled

Are we in the last days?
We, here, not far from the temple of anachronisms,
is time welling up out
of a natural spring with us trying to catch all
we catch in our hats?
It is a perfect day in November, but it might
be the day of Chronos
doing his eternal thing, leaving us to do ours.
Inquire of yourself: why
the despair? Why the migraines? If you were expecting
this poem to be a pearl,
you may want a refund. Me? I'm just my own bones, my
own cloth. I'm a compressed
sort of concubine, growing my parts into something
which may or may not rise,
but will most certainly burn. All of my moods suit me
fine and, while I do not
reflect the light as I used to, I still burn in it.

Publications

Non-Fiction

Lima Beans and City Chicken: A Memoir of the Open Hearth.
E.P. Dutton & Co. 1989

Poetry

An Apparent, Approachable Light
Chapbook, Astra Press 1998
Editor's Choice Prize

Running Like A Woman With Her Hair On Fire
Red Hen Press 2005

Not Untrue And Not Unkind
Arabesques Press 2006

After The Earthquake
Xlibris Publishing 2007

Perhaps You Could Breathe For Me
Xlibris Publishing 2009

Late Night Radio
Dog Ear Press 2010

What We Can't Forgive
Infinity Publishing 2011

Video Production
Writing and Direction

MediaVision
*California State Polytechnic University,
Pomona, California*

Poet's Series,
Coffee: Two Creams, No Sugar 1997

Daytime Drama,
Same River Twice 1998

Arts and Culture Series 2000-2003

Dance
Festival of Technology 2002

Achievements

Residency
Yaddo Artists Residency
1987

Pushcart Prize for Poetry
Nomination by Andrew Hudgins
1988

Residency
Djerassi Artists Retreat
1989

Residency
Anderson Center
Tower View Artists Retreat
1992

Editor's Choice
Chapbook Prize
Astra Press 1998

Reviews

Running Like A Woman With Her Hair on Fire,
Red Hen Press, 2005

David Fraser

JoSelle Vanderhooft

A Restless Experimenter With A Savvy Voice
After the Earthquake, Poems 1996-2006
Xlibris, 2007

Djelloul Marbrook

Not Untrue & Not Unkind by
Arabesques Press, 2006

Saul Landau

The Danger And Usefulness Of Poetry
Perhaps You Could Breathe For Me

Djelloul Marbrook

What We Can't Forgive
Infinity Press, 2011

Jeffrey Haste

Late Night Radio
Dog Ear Publishing, 2010

Jerry M Akron, New Review Books

Acknowledgements

Grateful acknowledgement is made to the following journals in which some of these poems first appeared.

Health Plan
Yet Another Small Magazine

No Hay Banda
Pedestal Magazine

Salutations and Prostrations
Arabesques War and Poetry Anthology

Praise
Saxifrage Press

Bad Manners
Cenacle Magazine

Postures
Best Poems Encyclopedia

All that Jazz and Bad Manners
Trivia Magazine

At the Polish Club
Another Cinco de Mayo
I Still Don't Know What I'm Celebrating
Atom Mind

Neutrinos
Snake Nation Review

Acknowledgements . . . *continued*

Front and Back Cover Photographs

Brian Newberry,
Brian Newberry Photography
Palm Springs, CA 92262
newberrymedia.com

Gratitude and Love to

William S. Peters, Sr., Editor/Publisher, Inner Child Press
Marcella Carri
Rick Cass
Sonia Chaidez
Hy Cohen
Alma de Melena Cox
David Fite
Kate Gale
Yolanda Gottlieb
Judih Weinstein Haggai
Deanna Hartman
K. Jacobvitz
Larry Kramer
Susan Kullman
Saul Landau
Djelloul Marbrook
Do Palma
Phillip Pommela
William Snead
Raymond Soulard
Phillip Spitzer
Michael Wilds

~ fini ~

www.ingramcontent.com/pod-product-compliance
Lightning Source LLC
Chambersburg PA
CBHW050800160426
43192CB00010B/1592